LIVING AN AUTHENTIC LIFE

Thomas E. Legere, Ph.D

Bloomington, IN Milton Keynes, UK

authorHOUSE®

AuthorHouse™
1663 Liberty Drive, Suite 200
Bloomington, IN 47403
www.authorhouse.com
Phone: 1-800-839-8640

AuthorHouse™ UK Ltd.
500 Avebury Boulevard
Central Milton Keynes, MK9 2BE
www.authorhouse.co.uk
Phone: 08001974150

First published by AuthorHouse 3/12/2007

ISBN: 978-1-4259-7865-5 (sc)

Library of Congress Control Number: 2006910019

Printed in the United States of America
Bloomington, Indiana

This book is printed on acid-free paper.

Acknowledgement

Biblical quotations in this manuscript are taken from <u>The Jerusalem Bible</u> (London, Darton, Longman & Todd, 1966), unless otherwise specified.

CONTENTS

FOREWORD

Living An Authentic Life is a book about seeking balance and harmony. We humans live out a complex juggling act between pleasure, power and meaning—this is our passage. Our desires for pleasure and power tie us to our instincts; our desire to understand, to find or create meaning tie us to the eternal. We need guides in this journey. Tom, like a well-informed guide, points out to us the things we in our busy lives (or because of our fears) look past. He asks that we travel with him on his lifelong journey to understanding, and build bridges along the way between that which is psychological and that which is spiritual. Allow yourself to step into the book as it works to blend the concepts of psychology into the world of spirit and show that the spirit is the core of our psychological makeup.

This book, though it rarely uses the word, is about transformation. We are asked to see how transformation is what faith and psychology have in common. Change is the gift that each has to give to us. Or as my mentor taught me, "To live is to change, to live well is to change often." We are creatures of change as Tom mentions in the section entitled, *The Breakdown Leading to a Breakthrough*, "…humans never stay the same. Within seven years every cell in our body changes."

But just as we seek change, we also resist change. There is a natural tension between the "Survival Personality" and the "Authentic Self."

In fact, Tom lays out well how we must go through and surrender parts of our survival personality to become authentic. As humans, half animal/half spirit, ours is a journey of transformation. The more we accept by stepping into this reality, the less we shame ourselves about the natural gifts and desires given to us, and the more energy we have to put toward spiritual growth.

The book in and of itself is a journey. Tom lays out for us the ways in which innocence makes us vulnerable; how from the loss of innocence we all experience, we start our journey of building defenses to protect ourselves and the false protection we may seek in money, sex, power, addiction, depression. Tom asked that we see these things as challenges, or perhaps better put, as our Higher Power knocking on our door asking us to offer up our beliefs in these inauthentic ways of walking through life in order to embrace our authentic self and in so doing taking a step or two closer to the Divine in all of us.

This book is a read that, like life, challenges one to think, feel, and be open to new perspective. Because of this, at times you will resist its message. Keep reading. Seek the breakthroughs that Tom sought. They are here—or at least parts of them can be found within these pages. Tom shares his story in hopes that it will help you to put together your own story so as to receive the gifts that are embedded within it. The energy we put into the inauthentic self is needed; it is to be given to The Divine, it is to become the path that we use to find higher ground. It is within our problems that our potential lies; it is within our potential we find our spirits, and within our spirits we find a meaningful life. This is the essence of Tom showing us that psychology and spirituality are not opposites but dear friends that, though separated by external circumstances, long to sit together and help each other have enjoyable and full lives. The pages of this book allow these friends a table to sit around, reconnect, enjoy their time together and enrich our lives. *Living An Authentic Life* invites us to pull up a chair, enjoy the dialogue, learn from it and make it part of our own.

Craig Nakken, MSW
Author of *The Addictive Personality*

INTRODUCTION

Let me begin with my rationale for writing this book. In the midst of a major personal crisis during the summer of 1976, I decided that I would not choose a spiritual path in life if it were not based on good psychological principles. Spirituality, for me, had to be based upon good psychology.

Over the ensuing years, I have managed to attain relative spiritual health without disregarding sound psychological principles. In the process, I have researched and charted what spiritual growth looks like from a psychological perspective. To the best of my knowledge, no one has specifically spelled out before the psychological steps involved in spiritual growth. Certainly, volumes have been written showing the *connection* between psychology and spirituality. In his own way, that is what Dante did centuries ago with the *Divine Comedy*. William James, the great American psychologist, broke ground in this area. So did Carl Jung, Viktor Frankl, and Rollo May. Contemporary researchers have also done amazing work in this regard. Ken Wilber, Frances Vaughan, Roger Walsh, John Firman, and others have all helped to make a case for the linkage between psychology and spirituality. However, I kept waiting for someone to lay out the whole process in a simple way that anyone can understand. This book is my attempt to do that.

Part of my task will entail sorting out some of the jargon that is being used so loosely these days. For example, spirituality is spoken about frequently. However, what exactly does the term mean and what does it imply we should do or be? This book will attempt to demystify the term and to explain in clear and simple terminology what spirituality means from a psychological perspective. Building on the research of those who continue to enlighten me, I will use my gift as a teacher to present a broad overview of what is to be expected on the spiritual path. This is the book I wished I had had in my possession when I went through the major turning points of my spiritual journey.

This book will trace each step of our conscious journey, to wholeness, which is divided into five major movements:

I. The Creation of the Inauthentic Self

II. How Inauthentic Living Brings Us Pain

III. The Death of the Inauthentic Self

IV. Discovering the Authentic Self

V. Living an Authentic Life

The individual chapters will then further explain these major themes as they usually unfold in the lives of most people. Notice the use of the qualifying words "usually" and "most". One always has to leave room for surprises and exceptions to the way people go through the journey, but the general movements of our growth in consciousness usually unfold according to a fairly predictable pattern. Joseph Campbell referred to the human race as the one hero with a thousand faces. By that he meant that the hero's journey unfolds according to a universal mythological pattern, but that each person goes through that process in their own unique way. Our journey generally follows a pattern that seems to be part of the "hard wiring" of the human race. Although this pattern can be discerned if one studies mythology, it is difficult to put into words.

One of my students summed up the process of spiritual growth this way. First, we are born with a spiritual connection. Then, as we grow up, we lose that sense of feeling connected to things eternal. We then try to fill up the hole that we feel within us with all sorts of things that do not work. Then our feeble efforts fail at filling up the hole within us. From a position of confusion and brokenness, we then rediscover that the truth has been within us all along. Then, if all goes according to plan, we live our lives according to whom we have always been all along.

The process of growing spiritually is actually a fairly simple one. However, simple does not mean easy. In fact, my own experience at rediscovering that the truth is within me was a traumatic process that I shall never forget.

Understanding intellectually what is happening to me has always been quite important for me. Perhaps it is a control issue. When I went through a major spiritual turning point back in 1976, I longed for someone who could explain what was happening to me. At 31 ½ years of age, I was at a point where I needed to let go of a narrow, ego-centered approach to life and see myself as part of something greater than myself. (See Figure 1)

Ego Centered Existence

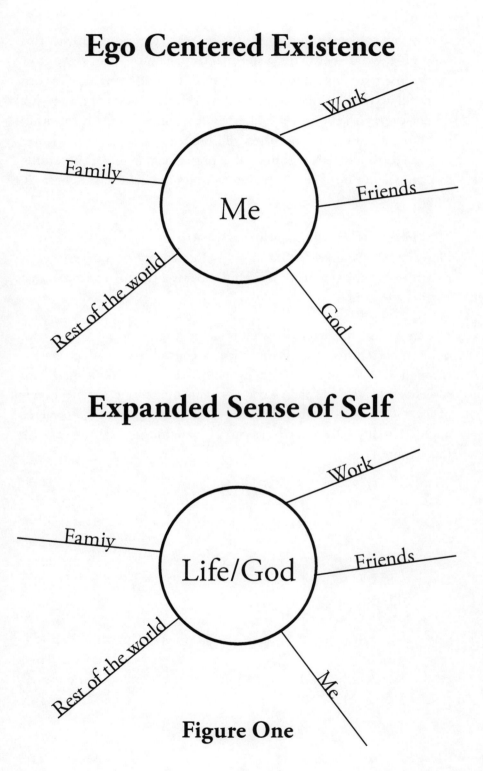

Expanded Sense of Self

Figure One

However, I did not understand what was happening to me at that time. I remember taking a course during that period, at Fordham University, entitled "The Psychology of Spirituality". I sat in the front row and took copious notes. One of my fellow students said, " Boy, you take the best notes of anyone I have ever seen." I replied, "For you, it may be a course. For me it is survival." I seem to remember her then looking at me like a side dish she didn't order.

At that time, I would have given my right arm if someone could have explained to me the meaning and purpose of my inner crisis. My book is an offering for all those who may find themselves in a similar crisis. *Understanding* what is happening can never be a substitute for taking the path. In fact, Freud called intellectualization one of the defense mechanisms of the ego. However, God must have given us the gift of intelligence for a reason. What is wrong with trying to understand something of the journey of faith? Saint Anselm actually defined theology as "faith seeking understanding." We can try to do a similar thing here: help make sense out of our inner journey.

So, to make some sense out of the spiritual journey, rather than using theology, which can cause people to retreat into rival camps, we will use psychology, a word that originally meant, "study of the soul". We will avoid dogma and anything smacking of religion. Religion can be helpful in some aspects of life, but I don't think it will be particularly helpful here. The basis of our explorations will not be abstract belief or theology, but *experience*. Only agree with something said here if you feel that it jibes with your experience. In fact, I pledge to the reader that I will not write anything that I have not personally struggled with myself.

The reader is encouraged to enter into the process of reading this book with trust and with courage. This book has entered your life for a reason. Our journey may stir up some unpleasant areas about our lives, but this kind of self-exploration may be the best move that we have ever made as adults. The truth will set us free. Let us begin by asking ourselves how and why we ever lost touch with our divine essence.

I. The Creation of the Inauthenic Self

CHAPTER ONE

Paradise Lost

The journey of life begins with perfection. In other words, we are born with a spiritual connection as part of our hard wiring. Our essence is divine. In order to get a feel for this, I will ask you to put aside your particular theological beliefs for a moment and trust your *experience* in life. What does your *experience* in life tell you about little babies? Isn't it your *experience* that these little souls are by nature

- Without fear

- Without guilt

- Without shame

- Without hang-ups

- Without neuroses

- Without body-hatred

- Without self-rejection

1

Isn't it also your *experience* that these innocent beings are, by nature:

- In awe

- Connected to their bodies

- Communicative of their needs

- Connected to nature

- Trusting

- Spontaneous

- Creative

- Joyful

Think of those little creatures and consider the fact that *you* were once so innocent and fearless as well. In other words, our confusion, alienation, and suffering are all learned behavior. None of it is innate. If you agree with this, then it will be clear that spirituality is not something that we so much "attain" as "recapture".

Every religion has some variation of a Garden of Eden story as a part of its teachings. Obviously, this is a story not about a geographical place nor about a time in history. This is a story about our own individual evolution in consciousness here in life. We all begin in a Garden of Eden, a state of consciousness where we have no need of clothing because we have not yet experienced shame. Our self-acceptance is total. Our communion with our parents is absolute. Psychologically, they are our gods.

Obviously, this state of blissful consciousness does not last for any of us. Part of the story is our expulsion from the Garden. We all can expect to lose this primal connection eventually, but we should keep in mind that we have all started on this journey in life from a position of perfection. Our journey as adults will not be to *become* spiritual, but to *rediscover* our spiritual core.

We are not talking here about regression or trying to roll back the clock and become infantile again. Our newly acquired consciousness over the years must be a part of the plan, too. We bring all that we have experienced with us on the spiritual journey. However, the answer to our questions is not outside ourselves; it is within. That is why the spiritual journey is often referred to as an "awakening" or an "unfolding." An authentic journey will not take us out of ourselves but deeper into ourselves. Yes, as you have intuited, the journey is within, and as mythologist Joseph Campbell puts it, "Eden *is*."

While on one level we are already perfect, already divine, we certainly do not, at the beginning of our conscious journey as adults, experience ourselves that way. In fact, our experience is often just the opposite. We feel estranged, cut off from our true selves. We are so far cut off from whom we really are that we have no conscious memory of our divine essence. We find it impossible to even *believe* that we are divine beings, let alone have any *experience* of this fact.

This experience of being cut off from our primal bliss is an eventuality for all of us. In that sense, our exile from Eden is inevitable. However, saying that the baby lives for the first five years or so of life in the Garden of Eden is not meant to be construed that the baby is a polished diamond yet. This precious baby still needs to be nurtured, reassured, taught, and molded. The baby is a masterpiece in the process of being created in its final form. However, saying that the diamond needs to be polished is a lot different than saying that the baby is fundamentally disordered. A diamond will always be a diamond. The baby may be an unpolished diamond, but it is far from being sinful and corrupt to the core.

This is no small point. There is a huge difference in how we treat a baby that we perceive as fundamentally good and whole and beautiful from a baby we perceive to be fundamentally corrupt. After having said I was going to avoid theology, please allow me one digression from my policy. I only make this digression because I think it is important. The issue has to do with the Christian dogma of original sin. From a psychological point of view, this dogma has done more to harm the mental health of the human race than anything that I can imagine. Think of its central premise: we are born fundamentally disordered and sinful. Having studied theology for four years at the Vatican, I am aware of the subtleties theologians make about this doctrine. However, those subtleties seldom filter down to the average person in the pew. For them, a central tenet of their faith states that something is fundamentally wrong with their babies. Watching the adoring looks they give to their newborns, parents seem to have some doubt about the inherent sinfulness of their babies. Still they dutifully bring their children to the Christening ceremony where they are reminded that their little ones are fundamentally flawed.

This book is not about theology. If you choose to believe the doctrine about original sin, fine. But can you possibly imagine how different our world would be if we saw our offspring as original *blessings* rather than originally *sinful*?

In any event, it is my experience, and perhaps yours as well, that there is a certain primal innocence and beauty about these little bundles from heaven. They come to us without any psychological wounds.

It is also our experience, however, that, sooner or later, we are all wounded by life. We experience what psychosynthesist scholar John Firman calls our "primal wound". This, most typically, is some experience of mistreatment that causes us to start shutting down and protecting ourselves. This is our first taste of fear, based on a felt sense that life is not totally safe. Not only does life have its dangers, but we sense that we cannot ever totally trust those who we were counting upon to defend us. (see Figure 2)

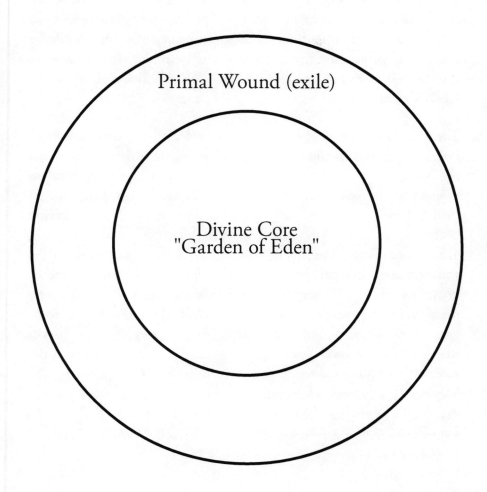

Primal Wound (exile)

Divine Core
"Garden of Eden"

Figure Two

There are many things that can cause our primal wound. For example, there may be objectively difficult moments in the young child's life like dealing with the death of one of its parents, or if the parents divorce. Or there may be what adults would objectively consider to be minor things like getting lost in a crowd for a few minutes or being dropped off at school for the first time amidst great tears and upset. While we adults may judge these things to be relatively minor, we can never be sure of their impact on the young child. What for one child would be inconsequential would for another child be traumatic.

The mistreatment can be either physical, emotional, mental or sexual. Perhaps the mistreatment actually happened or perhaps it was just the perception of mistreatment. It is not so crucial, in my opinion, to identify precisely what events, real or perceived, caused us to begin to shut down. Why do I say this? Because, in the end, perception becomes reality. It is impossible to get back to totally objective truth. What does matter very much, however, is what our *perception* of the situation was. Let me give an example. Frank McCourt, the author of *Angela's Ashes*, has been maligned in some circles by people who insist that things were not really as bad as he had portrayed them to be growing up as a little boy in Limerick, Ireland. But McCourt makes the point that this was how his life looked like as viewed through the prism of his childhood memories. His memoirs do not purport to be historically accurate. However, this is what it was like for him, and that is all that matters for him. Similarly, your memories conveyed to a therapist are *your* memories; they are *your* truth. As such, they need to be taken seriously.

While many traumatic things may happen to us in the course of our lives, there is often a special place in our memory about that first experience that life is not totally safe. What makes this primal wound so memorable is that, until that experience, we were under the assumption that life was on our side and that the big people in our lives could always be counted upon to protect us. However, then we may get lost in a crowd, or dropped on the floor by an adult, or put in a hospital where people in white clothes stick needles in us, or one of thousands of other scenarios. The common denominator in all of these possibilities is that we feel wounded by life for the first time. Most of us never forget this powerful subjective experience.

My own primal wound stands out very clearly for me. I was about seven or eight years old and my Dad was going to buy me a new baseball glove. He worked in downtown Philadelphia and I lived eight miles away in Somerdale, New Jersey. The plan was that my mom would put me on the bus in Somerdale and my dad would be there to meet me at Eighth and Market in Philadelphia. I can imagine what you are probably thinking. Put a little child on the bus alone for such a trip? Please remember that this was in the 1950's, truly an age of innocence in a lot of ways. That part of the story was not the problem.

When I got off the bus, my dad was not there to greet me. Not to worry. Mom had said that dad, my hero, would be there to meet me. If he was delayed a minute or two, just stay where you are. Your father will be there, she told me repeatedly. A half hour had passed. I was very worried. Actually, I was concerned from the moment I got off the bus. However, now the anxiety really began to rise in me. After forty-five minutes, I figured it was time to use the dime my mom had given me to make a phone call in case something went wrong. This call from a public phone was the first one I had ever made.

My mom explained on the phone that my dad showed up in Somerdale, not in Philadelphia. He had totally forgotten about our meeting. How could he have ever forgotten, I asked myself? It was all that I had thought about for a week. Mom told me to stay put and wait at the corner of Eighth and Market. Dad, who did not own a car, would take the bus back the fifteen miles to Philadelphia and meet me.

By the time he eventually arrived, I had been waiting for him for two hours. By now, the funkier element had begun to invade the street corner, and I had to go to the bathroom. I was one scared little kid.

It all turned out okay in the end, I guess. I got the best baseball glove in the store! It was the only time in my childhood that I ever heard my Dad say, "Get anything that you want." The poor guy had never let me down before and he never has let me down since that time.

However, this event contributed to my losing my innocent trust in life. Something in me began to shut down on that day. I got the message that even the people who love me may let me down sometimes. Adults are not omnipotent or God-like. Life is filled with dangers. Protect yourself and watch your back. You are in this alone. You cannot rely totally on anyone. Learn how to survive.

Demystifying Our Parents

As a counselor, I often hear clients defend the job that their parents did. I can understand this. I was always very defensive about my parents, too. They were "good enough", which is about the best any of us can ever hope to have on this earth. However, many clients resist any initial attempt to explore the client-parent relationship. They may respond: I come from a great family and our parents loved us very much. End of story.

For a client to admit that his or her parents were not 100% perfect, they may feel disloyal, insufficiently grateful for all the sacrifices their parents made for the family. Some clients defend these good people at all costs.

The only problem with this unconscious strategy is that it blocks us from dealing with our own wounds. We mistakenly believe that to acknowledge that we were wounded implies our parents must be at fault. The fact is that it is nobody's fault. No one is to blame. Even if our parents had something to do with our initial wounding, as was the case with myself, their part was often innocent and unintentional. They were usually doing the best that they could, and they simply were not capable of batting 1,000. Nobody is.

However, what of woundings that are apparently not so innocent? What of the beatings, neglect, sexual molestation, and emotional abuse that some have experienced? This is a little trickier to understand. Here we are not dealing with something so innocuous as a lapse in memory. Here we are dealing with something premeditated. To understand such abuse, go back to my original assumption. Everyone starts out as innocent, joyful, and creative. If this is the case, then something must have happened to our parents or other significant adult figures to make them behave the way they did. Were they mistreated themselves as children? Although we can never be certain, the research in the field seems to indicate that the abused often becomes the abuser. This is not an excuse or a justification; but it is, I think, at least an explanation.

A big part of our healing begins when we can demystify our parents. This means seeing them not primarily as our parents, but as human beings in need of our compassion. At times, too, they even need our forgiveness. We will visit this topic later, but for now it is crucial for us to face the limitations of the significant adults in our childhood. If we do not face the flawed humanity of our caretakers, we will never be able to face our own wounds and be healed.

The Many Wounds of Childhood

Every child is traumatized in some way. Though the trauma may not always be intentionally inflicted, the effect is the same. Innocence, spontaneity, and self-confidence are lost. The child now doubts his or her self-worth. The hallmarks of a spiritual being – joy, love, inner peace, creativity, and a sense of feeling connected with all things – is lost, either partially or totally. The young child now experiences fear for the first time. The world is now not experienced as a safe place. Cast out of that psychological state that we call the Garden of Eden, the child forgets about his or her divine origin. Those connections are a distant memory now. The stage is set for a lifetime of trying to reconnect again with a sense of our divine essence.

When we speak about the primal wound, there can be a tendency to think everything that has gone wrong can be traced back to some single, traumatic event. That is probably not the case. Instead, there were recurring *themes* that shaped us. Over weeks, months and years, life and its experiences shaped us in certain ways. The shaping took place as a result of the deeply ingrained attitudes of our primary caretakers. Very little harm was ever probably done to us in any conscious way. We just absorbed the brokenness and wounding of all of those around us. Unresolved issues that pass down from one generation to the next opened wounds in us.

The fact that our wounding results more from a *theme* rather than a single *event* is why I do not try to dig too deeply in therapy for the one event that started a client's ills. If there was such an event, can we ever find it? Is it all that important to identify it? I do not think so. The bottom line is that every human being who walks the face of the earth has been traumatized in one way or the other. This trauma affects us profoundly and sets up our hunger and thirst to rediscover our original wholeness.

Please note that the divine essence has not gone anywhere, except underground in the unconscious. In other words, we are and always will be spiritual beings no matter what happens to us. All that is lost is the *awareness* of that divinity.

We lose that awareness in many ways. In his book, *Character Styles*[1], psychologist Steven Johnson lists seven different patterns that can cause children to lose that divine consciousness. All involve some mistreatment by adults, due to their brokenness or inadequacy. We hear different messages from our caretakers and consequently we are all wounded in different ways.

The *hated* child picks up the most frightening message of all: you do not have a right to exist. This message can produce a schizoid personality. This deeply conflicted and divided person will always feel like a stranger in a strange land.

The *abandoned* child never got the constant and unconditional love that it needed in the very first years of life. Because the caretaker was often absent - either physically or emotionally – the child never had its most basic needs met. Consequently the message that this child picked up was that it is not OK to have needs. This child comes to believe that his or her needs are not legitimate.

The *owned* child has never really been encouraged to be him or herself. Identified with the parents, this child idealizes the parents to such an extent that it thinks that to be oneself is to somehow hurt the caregiver. The message here is that I am an extension of my parents. My job is not to be myself but to make them proud of me.

The *used* child has been unconsciously manipulated by the caregivers. The caregivers have set things up in such a way that the child believes that it can do no wrong. Like a performing seal, the youngster gets the message that if he does all the right things, then he will be loved. Frequently very capable, the youngster grows up with a narcissistic personality structure. In this instance, the child gets the message that, "I am not real. You are not real. You are an object to me. I am an object to you. We use, manipulate, and play with each other. We do not connect. We do not feel, we do not love. We are machines who use each other in the mechanical process of getting through the day and night." (Johnson, p. 165).

The *defeated* child has had its efforts at self-expression squashed at every turn. Everything she does is met with disapproval. All initiatives are blocked. Sooner or later, this child quits even trying. The child resigns herself to the fact that she has no control over life, no ability to carve out any way but the way of her caretakers. The message here is: you will submit to the will of us adults or you will be beaten into submission.

The *exploited* child has been taken advantage of by those who are supposed to care for him or her. The exploitation can come in everything from using the child as a slave to do the parents bidding to being a sexual object to take care of the adult's needs. Rather than being "blessed" by the elders, this child focuses on meeting others' needs.

The *disciplined* child has learned how to follow rules to a tee. The learning comes in all sorts of ways. Perhaps it is the fear of punishment, the fear of having love withheld, or the fear of offending an earthly or a heavenly deity. The bottom line is that this youngster grows up (or does not grow up, depending on one's point of view) knowing how to follow the rules of life to a tee. Later in life a candidate for obsessive-compulsive behavior, the internalized message is: I should be perfect.

Perhaps you can find yourself or elements of yourself in one or more of these neurotic patterns that Dr. Johnson has so clearly laid out. I know I certainly can. All of these neurotic patterns, that developed in us through no fault of our own, have thrown us off from our sense of feeling divinely connected. This is how the spiritual path begins for all of us. We feel like we have lost that innate sense of perfection and divinity and have acquired a fear-based attitude towards life. We can still manage to limp along, but we are far from operating at our best. Eventually as we grow up we develop this thing called an "ego", which is an individual sense of self. Designed to be the servant of the soul, the ego is not supposed to cause us troubles, but, because of our wounds, it almost invariably does. Our next chapter will trace the origins of the ego and show how a disordered ego can set us up for a lot of pain and hopefully for an eventual journey home to our spiritual magnificence.

CHAPTER TWO

What About the Ego?

What exactly is the ego and how does it get formed? More importantly, what is the relevance of the ego- if anything- to the spiritual path? Does the child, with that mystical consciousness of the Garden of Eden, have an ego? Or is the ego something that develops later in life?

The word "ego" comes from the Latin and simply means "I". It is without content, without baggage, and without fear. It is the witness. The ego gives us a sense of being an individual, separate self. There is nothing negative about it. I am defining ego the way Freud does, and the way in which Jung uses it when he refers to the "little self". Freud used the word ego as a substitute for the self. Jung made a distinction between the self in the everyday world (ego) and one's "higher Self," a term which he uses to refer to our soul or essence. (see Figure 3) I realize that some of these distinctions concerning the ego can be confusing at first. So let us agree on what we mean by the various terms. The word ego is synonymous, then, with our "little self" (Carl Jung). To refer to the ego with a fully expanded consciousness we will use the terms soul, Self, big Self (Jung), or Higher Self.

Synonyms for the Ego
and the Soul

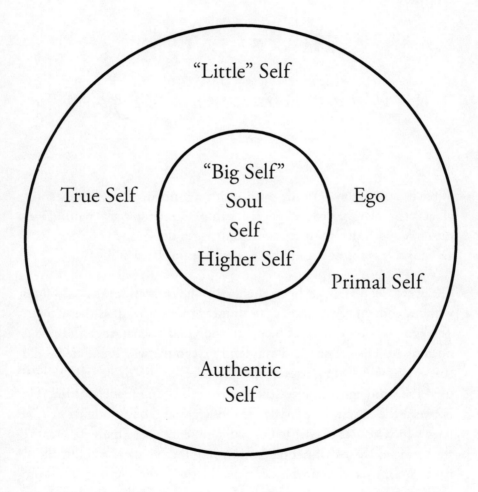

Figure Three

The ego emerges during the first few years of life. In the beginning, the baby does not even realize that it is a separate creature from its mother. If all goes well, the child will be taught that he or she has an independent existence.

The development of a healthy ego is essential to our mental and spiritual health. Spiritually healthy people have healthy egos. For example, can you think of anyone with a healthier ego, a stronger sense of self than Jesus of Nazareth? Here was a person who had confidence in himself and his teachings, who was not a people pleaser, and was not afraid of being criticized. He had an enormously strong ego. One could say the same thing about Martin Luther or Martin Luther King Jr. Certainly Moses would be another strong example. So would Mother Teresa. These people all had an aura of self-confidence and strength about them. However, to use Jung's terminology, their egos were always at the service of their Higher Self. The ego makes a wonderful servant, but can be a tyrannical master. When it is serving the soul, everything is in perfect order. Its role is to be the good soldier and to carry out the orders of the soul, to report to duty each day and say, "Here I am. Use me in whatever way you want."

As long as the ego remembers its place, everything works smoothly. Things only go wrong when there is revolution within the ranks, and the good soldier now tries to be a dictator. Chaos results.

We are all familiar with the *egocentric* person. This person puts their ego where the soul should be, namely, at the center of the universe. In both instances, the person needs a spiritual Copernican revolution. Their ego, a planet of the soul, needs to get back into its own orbit.

Putting the planet back into its orbit and the soldier back into the ranks is not the same thing as destroying the planet or killing the soldier. We are not served well by a destroyed ego; but by a healthy and strong ego that knows its place.

I feel so passionately about this subject because I have witnessed and experienced the shaming of people's sense of self. Young children, in particular, and adults, as well, are often made to feel guilty about having thoughts, opinions, and feelings. As Steven Johnson pointed out in Chapter One, some children are hated or abandoned or owned. Others are used, defeated, exploited, or inappropriately disciplined.

Certainly, to one degree or the other, we have all been wounded. This wound has led, in turn, to the formation of a fear-based survival personality. That unhappy chain of events will be addressed in Chapter Three. But the point here is that step number one in life is to develop as healthy a sense of the little self, or ego, as possible. Everything else follows from that.

I have often had to remind clients of this fact, especially those in too big of a hurry to *transcend* the ego. Sure, the essence of the spiritual life is to surrender, to give yourself away to a Higher Power, but, first of all, you must own a sense of self in order to give it away! Before giving themselves away, people need to know who it is that they are transcending. Jumping into transcendence before having a sense of self puts the cart before the horse.

The necessary and appropriate role of the ego in spiritual growth is often overlooked. People frequently use the term in a negative way. In the Twelve Step Philosophy, for example, you may hear people say that the word ego is an anagram that stands for "ease God out." Today, ego is often written about in a pejorative way, as if the ego was the source of all evil.

In point of fact, the ego is not the enemy of spiritual growth, but a prerequisite for it. Our sense of self, of ego, is initially quite limited. In the very beginning of life, the baby does not even know that it is a different being from the mother. Then the child slowly develops a sense of the little self, or ego, as being separate and unique. Eventually, however, the ego's challenge is to keep expanding its consciousness from identification with the body to an adult sense of being a part of all things, even to being a part of God. In order to make this journey successfully, one needs a solid base, a good sense of self, however limited this might be, as a foundation. On the level of ontology, of being, our ego is already divine. However, the mind's journey to Buddha consciousness, to Christ consciousness, presumes a healthy ego that can keep expanding to the point where it can *claim* its divine birthright.

When some people speak about killing or eliminating the ego, they are confusing the individual sense of the little self, the ego, from other distorted aspects of ourself. Certainly those distorted parts need to be dealt with, but the ego per se is not the enemy. If our primal identity is divine, then why would we ever wish to destroy that? In trying to eliminate the ego, as many spiritual authors want us to do, it seems to me that we are creating a recipe for disaster. It is setting up a needless war within the self, virtually guaranteeing a neurosis.

In dialoguing about his subject with some of my academic peers, I have struck by the depth of feelings around this subject. Some understand the important distinctions I am trying to make, and why I am trying to make them. Others feel that our ego is almost synonymous with the devil. It represents, for them, the inner adversary, the enemy of spiritual growth. How can we account for these differences of perspective?

As you will see as you read on in this book, I often find it helpful to go back to the original meaning of words. I have already mentioned earlier in this chapter that the word "ego" comes from the Latin and meads "I", the first person singular pronoun of the infinitive "to be". Note here that this word in English, "I", is capitalized. It seems to me that this is recognition that a person can be capable of speaking from the most noble, even divine, part of who they are. There is a part of us that, in a best case scenario (e.g. Jesus, Buddha, the saints), can be a clear channel of divine consciousness. When we are speaking from the part of who we are, we speak the truth as pure sons and daughters of God.

In popular parlance, however, we also sometimes use the word "me". Note that, in English, the word "me" is in the lower case, unlike the word "I". When we are speaking from the vantage point of our "me" state of consciousness, we are on an entirely different frequency. "Me" – thinking is fear-based and thinks in terms of separateness. This is the "unworthy" part of us that is in "sin" ("missing the ,mark" in greek); this is the part of us that contributes to the disorder in our world.

Clearly, this wounded part of us is not in alignment with divine consciousness. This part of us is in need of "redemption". This part of us truly is, in some sense, the enemy within. The Saint Pauls, the Martin Luthers and the John Calvins of the world have a point. We are often so blinded by the "me" that we cannot any longer see the "I". Or, even worse, we begin to think that the "me" is the "I".

The disaster of living according to "me" consciousness is an important point to make. But I think it is crucial to also make the point that our fundamental identity as human beings, our essence if you will, is beautiful and perfect and divine. The "I am" consciousness, the ego state before its wounding, is not the problem. Our problem is the "inner adversary", the "me" that thinks it has an independent existence apart from God.

Hopefully these clarifications will prove to be helpful. I am not naïve. I am acutely aware of how blinded we are. But I maintain that originally our consciousness was not blinded and, by the grace of God, can be that way once again. To summarize: while being "me"-centered is part of the problem, the recovery of a sense of "I" is our only hope of living an authentic life.

Splitting

I suspect that right about now the reader is experiencing mixed feelings. Part of us recognizes the truth of everything written in this chapter. However, another part of us feels like it is cut off from divine consciousness. This part of us feels like we are all tied up in knots, confused, and unhappy. How did we get this way?

In the previous chapter, we learned about some of the ways that our ego, our sense of self, gets hammered early in life. Each blow chips off awareness of part of our primal essence, banished into the unconscious. In extreme cases, the little self is pulverized into psychosis or it is split in two (dissociative disorder). Sometimes, people are severely damaged by childhood trauma, yet they can still manage to function relatively well on the surface (borderline personality disorder).

Normally, we have a relatively solid ego structure (no psychosis, major splitting, or borderline indications), yet we may feel like we are at war within ourselves. There are competing "voices" heard within. If the voices are heard literally, outside oneself, then we are experiencing hallucination, indicative of a mental illness. However, for us everyday neurotics, there is none of that. The individual appears normal in every way. Though fully functioning, the person still feels a lack of harmony due to lack of inner integration. Our lack of harmony comes from the fact that our little self, our ego, has been split in some way. The parts of us that have been split off never really disappear; they just live in the unconscious. (see Figure 4)

Parts of the Ego "Banished" into our Personal Unconscious

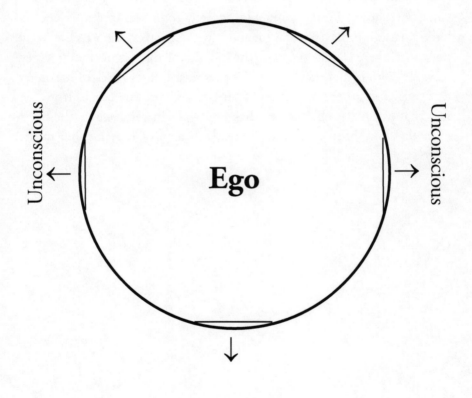

Figure Four

Let us try to summarize what we have said so far about the spiritual journey:

1. The little self and the Higher self are both divine and, therefore, perfect.

2. The newborn soul of the child initially <u>reflects</u> that divine perfection.

3. Some <u>wounding</u> to the ego of the child most typically by its primary caregivers, causes the child to lose its sense of innocence.

4. There are many ways to be wounded, but they all result in the person feeling fear and a lack of safety.

5. This expulsion from the Garden of Eden results in our alienation.

6. While we are already whole and perfect in our innermost core, very few of us feel that way.

Living in what we increasingly perceive to be an unsafe world, feeling afraid and unsafe, we need to find a way to survive. In our next chapter, we will see how most of us human beings cope by creating a "survival personality."

CHAPTER THREE

I Will Survive: The Creation of the Survival Personality

The very first mandate for all life is to survive. Survival is programmed into our genes and chromosomes. Its impulse arises from the deepest layer of our brain, the medulla oblongata, the brain stem, commonly called the reptilian brain. Beneath the patina of respectability that we show the world, our drive to live is supreme. We will do whatever we have to do to avoid being swallowed up by life itself.

The survival drive is unconscious. We are not usually aware that we are responding to it. We may deny the primacy of this drive since it does not sound civilized or spiritual. However, make no mistake, if you are an adult reading this passage, then you have somehow developed survival skills that have enabled you to fend off life's onslaughts. You have been smart or cunning, and have unconsciously figured out a way not to be destroyed by life's pains and challenges.

A person who is so suspicious and so defensive and feeling under attack is a person living in fear. This fear is chronic and not related to anything in particular. This is not situational fear, which is explainable by the fact of an imminent danger to your organism. If you are attacked by a lion or assaulted by an armed robber, fear is a perfectly appropriate response. When facing imminent danger, fear protects the organism. Nothing strange there. However, that is not the kind of fear being dealt with here. Instead, we are talking about free-floating or ontological fear, the kind that is not specific to any particular situation, but is with us twenty-four hours a day. It colors the way we treat other people (what does this person want from me?). It colors the way we make decisions about life (what will probably go wrong?). And, finally, it colors the basic attitude we have about life itself (is life on my side or not?). This chronic, all pervasive fear-based attitude toward being a human being starts early in life, usually within the first five years.

While it is true that youngsters are still living "in the Garden" during their first five years, the world is still capable of invading the Garden and wounding them. In fact, the developmental psychologists are in general agreement that the personality is formed *by the age of five*. That is what makes the wounding so insidious. It robs children of their early years which are meant to be years of innocence.

The Survival Personality

Psychosynthesist scholars John Firman and Ann Russell coined the term survival personality.[2] The survival personality refers to the fear-based, constricted, pain-producing personality pattern that gets in the way of our spiritual growth. They meant this term to apply to all human beings at this stage of our evolution. In other words, we are all at least slightly wounded and therefore all at least slightly neurotic. Sure, it is theoretically possible to be perfectly well adjusted, but have any of us ever met anyone who was?

The term survival personality makes it clear that the problem causing our psyche pain is not the ego, but, rather, this shame-based, fear-based creation that cuts us off from reality, rather than helping us embrace it.

When we have been wounded deeply by the pains of life, especially the first time, then a whole part of us begins to shut down. What had been a child who is innocent and in awe, trusting, spontaneous, creative, and joyful, now becomes an organism which feels attacked. Out of this primary fear-based attitude towards life, we develop a survival personality. (see Figure 5)

Personality is a combination of that within us which is innate (genes, temperament, and type) along with our character (the person that we choose to become). The origin of the word personality comes from the Latin word *persona*, which means mask. In other words, we put on a false face that we show to the world. We all wear masks at times, and that is not necessarily unhealthy at all. For example, we may put on the persona of wife, mother, or teacher, and act accordingly. There is nothing unhealthy about this, as long as we can take off the mask when appropriate. We may put on our mom mask and act protectively, our wife mask and act romantically, or our teacher mask and act pedantically. So far so good. The masks are functional and are meant to be optional and interchangeable.

When the ancient Greeks put on plays, the actors would usually wear masks. However, at the end of the play, they would always come out before the audience, take off their masks, and reveal their identities. This benefited the audience and the actors. The audience would not continue to project the actor's role onto the actor and the actors could disidentify from the roles that they had been playing.

When we can take off our masks and disidentify from them, all is well. But if the mask gets stuck on our face, we are in trouble. In certain jobs, there is a tendency for people to overly identify with the roles that they are playing. They may have a hard time stepping away from their roles and being themselves. For example, a mom may not know what to do with herself after her children are raised. Or a drill sergeant may have a tough time stepping out of his or her role at the end of the day. Many politicians find it incredibly difficult to leave the limelight and bow out of political life. It is often difficult for members of the clergy to shed their clerical attire, step down from their pulpit, and just be themselves, whether on a vacation or in retirement.

The Survival Personality Emerges from the Primal Wound

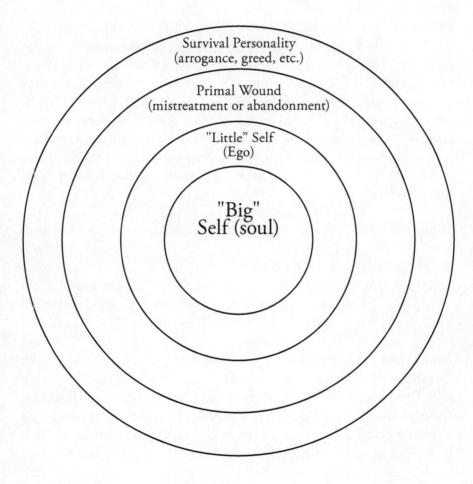

Survival Personality
(arrogance, greed, etc.)

Primal Wound
(mistreatment or abandonment)

"Little" Self
(Ego)

"Big"
Self (soul)

Figure Five

These are all fairly clear examples, I think, of how identifying with a role, with its subsequent mask, can be psychologically dangerous. But the survival personality we are talking about here is much more deeply ingrained than whatever roles we may be playing. It goes much beyond what job we may be holding in life. It goes to the heart of our self concept. Years, usually decades, have gone into the unconscious construction of our fear-based sense of our ego. It will then logically take an elaborate "demolition job" for the person to discover the treasures buried beneath their very limited sense of who they are.

Why, you ask? Why is it so difficult to find the true self, once the survival personality has taken a place of prominence? The reason is simple and devastating: the individual has no felt sense that there is anything anymore beneath their mask. Not only is there no felt sense of interiority and self worth; there is no belief that any exists. All of us are, to one degree or the other, shame-based. Author John Bradshaw maintains that guilt is feeling badly about what we have *done*. He sees this as a healthy thing. However, he says that shame is feeling badly about whom we *are*. This is clearly a neurotic pattern, indicative of a person at war within himself.[3]

Certainly the wounding of the psyche is more extreme with some people than with others. Also the patterns of the survival personality are more deeply ingrained in some more than others. However, I would maintain that our wounding has made us all at least slightly neurotic. A life based on love, peace, and joy seems like an impossible dream to all those still locked in their old patterns of fear.

I remember once a man telling me that he had not been leveling with me about what sort of person he really was. On this occasion he was finally choosing to come clean with me. He leaned towards me in a conspiratorial manner and said, "Deep down, I am no good." It was as if he was revealing a long suppressed secret about himself. Finally, he bared his soul and told the ultimate truth about how he felt about himself.

I was not impressed. Of course, I was aware that there were wheels within wheels in this man's personality, just as there are with everyone. Obviously, I had known for a long time before that this man was not as perfect as he had been pretending to be. However, what I knew and he did not was that a beautiful soul existed deep within him. This inner core had been totally covered over with barnacles. There was no longer a belief, let alone an experience, of this treasure buried within a field. The man was left with the all too common belief that he was, as the expression goes, "rotten to the core."

This belief about oneself rises out of a deep shame that is found in many people. If people feel so badly about who they are, no wonder they wear their masks, their persona, so tightly. No wonder they will do almost anything to resist taking it off. No wonder they will not let anyone get a glimpse of who or what is behind the mask. They think that perhaps there is a monster within, so, naturally, they do not let the world get even a peek behind the mask.

Is it any wonder that there is such a fear of intimacy with so many people? One of the reasons that people will not let others behind their hard exterior is that they are often ashamed of who they are. This reluctance extends even to one's significant other. The image of perfection must be upheld at all costs. Their great fear is that if anyone ever saw behind the mask, they would be horrified. If the person herself is horrified by what is there, what would others think?

Some Common Survival Personalities

Another helpful metaphor to explain our fear-based way of relating to the world is the term "dragon", used by José Stevens. In his book, Transforming Your Dragons, Stevens never mentions or alludes to the term survival personality. However, it seems to me that he is using the term in roughly the same way Firman does when he is talking about the survival personality. Both terms – "survivor personality" and "dragon" indicate, it seems to me, that we are far from being at peace within ourselves. So we will use the terms synonymously in this chapter. The names of the seven dragons come from Stevens. However, the patterns described are as old as the human race. The description of these survival personalities, these dragons, is mine. (see Figure 6)

1. Arrogance – The American Heritage Dictionary defines the arrogant person as one "overly convinced of one's own importance; overbearingly proud; haughty."[4] There is often present in the arrogant person a sense of supreme self-confidence. They appear to be absolutely sure of who they are and what they believe. Actually, if you scratch the surface of the arrogant person, you will often find a person who is deeply insecure.

Carl Jung explains this by what he calls enantriodroma, a term referring to the fact that the psyche tends to swing to an extreme when seeking to come into balance. Jung's mentor Freud would explain this as a "reaction formation." This concept implies that when we are afraid of a certain reaction of ours, we will develop and show to the world the opposite reaction. Of course, this reaction is unconscious.

Though the arrogant person, then, is filled with fear, let us speak a word of defense for this survival personality. It, as all survival personalities, enables the individual to survive. This is no small thing. All survival personalities always contain a gold nugget, something worth saving. In the case of the arrogant type, the gold nugget is self-confidence. In its undiluted form, arrogance is toxic. However, many people could use a bit of this personality pattern. For example, those persons who are not assertive enough could benefit some from the bravado and braggadocio of the arrogant person.

This person has the confidence and often the ability to get things done. The problem for arrogant people is not that they do not have much to offer to the world. Clearly they do. It is just that their contributions are being made at too high a personal cost to themselves. Their deep sense of insecurity is with them constantly, even as they try to project just the opposite to the world. Out of touch with the true self, they experience personal anguish and often unintentionally inflict it upon others as well.

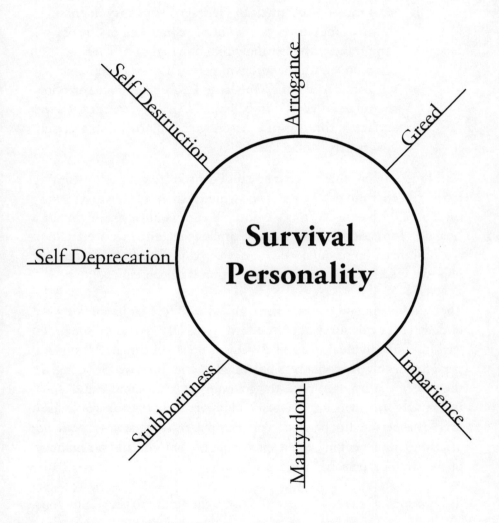

Figure Six

2. Greed – Greedy people try to protect themselves from
   their inner pain by accumulating money, things, ideas
   or pounds. They hope that these things will serve as
   insulation, a protective barrier from feeling their feelings.
   If there are enough layers of defense, so the unconscious
   thinking goes, life will not be able to get to them.

The gold nugget with greed is that at least these persons will be able to
support themselves. Many other people cannot do so and they could
use just a little bit of what the greedy person has. The goal is not for
anyone to literally *become* a greedy person. That would be substituting
a vice for an insufficiency. However, there are some people in the world
who have great difficulty in sustaining themselves materially. They
could benefit from some of the worldly skills of the greedy person.

Perhaps at this time you are asking yourself the question: "Why do
people develop different survival personalities?" The answer goes back
to our earliest childhood experiences and our first role models. For
example, a young man may develop an arrogant subpersonality because
he sees how apparently successful his father has been with that approach
to life. He sees his father intimidate others and get away with it. So
why not do the same thing? It appears to get results.

There may be some minimal amount of free will that determines which
path we go down, but there is not much. Like romantic love, which
chooses us rather than we choosing it, the circumstances of our life
usually have us heading down a particular path before we know it.
Perhaps the role models in our lives got the ball rolling in a particular
direction. Or perhaps we discovered that a particular pattern – let's say
playing the martyr – got us some of what we wanted in life. However,
very little of how things developed in our psyche was conscious. At
most times the patterns were well in place long before we even knew
that there was a pattern.

One way the greed dragon sometimes manifests itself is through what
has traditionally been called gluttony. The glutton is trying to fill his

or her stomach in the same way that the greedy person is trying to fill his or her bank account. Both have this much in common: they are trying to take away their inner pain through some substance extraneous to themselves. However, the simple truth of the matter is that no thing can ever fill up that God-sized hole that we all have in our hearts.

I have a wonderful example of how this pattern developed in my family of origin. My dad worked for the federal government most of his life. In those days, government employees made very little money. In addition, working mothers were more the exception than the rule. So my dad had to try very hard to feed his family, which included three growing boys and a girl. Things were so tight financially that my dad had a lock put on our refrigerator to keep us hungry kids from foraging for food.

This was particularly tough for my brother John, the biggest of us all. He went on to become an all-state football player and attended West Point on a football scholarship. However, as a little kid, he could never seem to get enough to eat. As a result, he developed the greed dragon in order to make sure that he always got his piece of the pie. Not that he is literally greedy. He is not. However, he makes sure that he will never again be "locked out" from what he wants in life.

> 3. Impatience – The individual who develops this particular subpersonality will always be on the move, rushing about, consumed by trivialities and distractions. He or she will have a hard time living in the present and will never really be able to enjoy what has been done. Like a trained seal jumping through hoops or a rat on a treadmill, he or she will never be able to rest.

For this person, time is a precious commodity, a thing, and there is never enough of it.

Never present to the here-and-now, the individual relentlessly careens towards the future. Where do I have to be? What do I have to do? When will I ever be able to do it all? Uptight and tense, the impatient person can not enjoy a vacation, meditate, or even be an attentive lover, because reality is divided into units, each unit must end with an accomplishment, and events like vacations, meditation, or love making do not really "accomplish" anything.

The quality of life for such an individual is very low. Never satisfied with what is, edgy, irritable, and on the move, the impatient person is unable to be present to themselves or to one another.

What is this dragon, this survival personality, really all about? Remember, all dragons are, in essence, about the same basic thing: trying to dull the pain of feeling empty inside. This particular dragon tries to alter this feeling of emptiness by always being on the move. There is an old expression: it is hard to hit a moving target. When you are always living in the future, then perhaps you will not feel your current pain.

When we go deeper into the core of this dragon, we find a human being with a deep sense of existential shame, a sense that the person is devoid of any inherent value. Feeling so utterly empty inside, the person copes by acting as a human "doing" rather than a human "being." If I am always on the move accomplishing and achieving, I will be able to dull the inner ache by deluding myself that I have value, after all, because of what I have done. I will be able to step back and look at myself and conclude that maybe I am not as bad as I feel. After all, how could anyone who is so conscientious and productive be so bad?

I know this dragon very well, from the inside out. I discovered early on in life that if I accomplished much, I would be rewarded by praise from all of the people whose love and approval I sought. Each day, each minute, each second, was not to be wasted. Each unit of time gave me a chance to validate my existence. Even now, as a fully-grown and seasoned man, I feel driven to push on and climb my latest "Everest."

The gold nugget in such a personality pattern is that this is the type of person who gets things done in life. These are the movers and shakers who make the world go around. The dysfuntionality comes in that the person never, ever really feels OK about whom they are. Each triumph is short-lived. Before the congratulatory bottle of champagne is finished, the individual has jumped in their minds on to the next project. Will there ever be enough time to do it all? Of course not. Until the spiritual hunger within is eventually addressed, the treadmill keeps on running.

> 4. Stubbornness – The stubborn person puts his or her foot down and says "no" to any proposal. They do so before considering the relative merits of the proposal in question. Their knee-jerk reaction to any proposal is always "No".

Needless to say, it can be very difficult dealing with such a person. They are the obstructionists in life, the foot draggers. They never think any suggestion is a good one, any arrangement fair, or any proposal worth considering. They are the last ones to go along with anything and the first to complain.

At first glance, it is difficult to find the "gold nugget" in this survival personality. Where did it come from and what does it offer? If we examine the origin of this pattern, it probably started with a little child who felt manipulated and pushed around. It is important to remember that perception is everything in life, especially to a little child. In the land of the giants, every adult wish or command probably seems overwhelming to the child. This youngster most probably had no felt sense of boundaries. She may have been touched roughly, picked up when she did not want to be, tickled to the point of tears, kissed by adults with alcohol on their breath, and ordered to do things that were felt to be difficult or at least unfair.

This little child learned the strategic importance of putting down one's foot and slowing up the proceedings before they got out of hand. This is not such a bad quality to have cultivated in life. While domination by this pattern brings suffering, there are many of us who could use a little more of this energy. Perhaps we skipped over the terrible twos and the rebellious teens, and always went along with almost anything that was asked of us.

No one ever asked these types what they wanted to do, let alone what they thought. They felt carried along by other people's choices and expectations. Perhaps they were actually afraid to say "no". They wanted to be the good boy or good girl and always did what was expected, whether or not it was in their best interest. This sort of person could actually stand to have just a little bit of this stubborn energy.

Putting one's foot down is a way of getting some control in life, or at least feeling like one has some control. The difficulty comes not in its origins, but with its long-term consequences. What started out as a child trying to gain some manageability in life ends up as an adult whose life has become unmanageable because of a tight, negative, unyielding, cynical attitude toward whatever is suggested by anyone at any time and in any place. With all due respect to the salvageable aspects of this personality pattern, its grip needs to be broken.

>   5. Self deprecation – We all know this pattern well. It belongs to the person who is always putting himself down. This individual will always find something wrong with himself. All compliments, even sincere and well earned ones, are immediately deflected. Accomplishments, if they ever happen, are written-off and denigrated. The individual minimizes every accomplishment and beats himself up because it could always have been done better.

This dragon is a particularly insidious one because of the inner programming factor. If you tell yourself something often enough, it will probably come true. In other words, negative self-talk often becomes a self-fulfilling prophecy. If this dragon is not slain early in life, it will be very difficult to dislodge later in life. Speech patterns and thought patterns and energy patterns will become deeply ingrained. The unlearning process may take years, sometimes decades.

This assumes, of course, that the individual might want to change the patterns. However, why change the patterns if they seem to be working? Our patterns might be neurotic and self-defeating in the long run, but we employ them because we think that they will work for us. To some extent, they do work. We are at least under the impression that these patterns are working. Otherwise, why would we employ them?

At first glance, this pattern seems as worthless as the stubbornness pattern. What possible good could come from it? People berate themselves twenty-four hours a day and refuse to be positively acknowledged or complimented. What do such individuals get from such an attitude and from such behavior? First of all, they get attention. Persons who have minimized their contributions will end up getting more compliments in the long run than anyone else. People are always telling them, "You don't realize how much you have to offer"; or "You are a beautiful person, you just don't realize it." So there is the factor of positive feedback. Of course, if a person is shame-based, no amount of positive affirmation will ever satisfy the dragon. Such an individual will always feel inadequate.

The second payoff for this individual is very subtle. Those suffering from self-deprecation will never disappoint or let down anyone in life. How is this accomplished? It is accomplished by unconsciously communicating from the very beginning the message, "Don't expect anything out of me. I'm telling you this beforehand. I am a loser. I will fail. I will never accomplish anything worthwhile. Next question."

In a strange kind of way, then, the self-deprecating individual is the only one who will never fail to meet the expectations of others because the bar for success has been placed so low. No success is expected; no success is attained; and no one is surprised.

Is there anything worthwhile in this ostensibly pitiful pattern of living? Of course. For one thing, at least the individual is not grandiose. At least the self-talk is not always centered on how spectacular the individual is. The arrogant person may look in the mirror and sing,

"How Great Thou Art." The self-deprecating individual would never contemplate such a thing. They do have a form of humility, however distorted it might be. In the end, the humility is false because real humility is truth. However, it is true that at least the individual does not focus everything on himself.

As mentioned earlier, this dragon will not be an easy one to slay. However, it can be done. It may take an eruption from deep within one's unconscious to reveal the true self, but the good news is that there is hope for all those beset with this dragon.

> 6. Martyrdom – All dragons are cunning. None show their true face at first. This dragon is no exception. For the person who plays the role of the martyr may look at first like a saint. This even may appear on the surface to be a psychologically healthy individual, operating out of the true self, fulfilling a spiritual call. However, on closer inspection, what is actually there is a manipulative individual, deeply self-centered, trying to control his environment by reaching out for attention and admiration.

A distinction needs to be made here. There are loving servants in the world. Altruism is possible. People can do things out of genuine care for others. Such healthy individuals, however, serve others from a sense of their own abundance. Their primary needs are met, and now they desire to help others. That is a far cry from the fear-based individual who acts in an apparently loving way, but actually is doing so out of a deep sense of inferiority. In that instance, the good deeds are employed as a way of papering over what feels like a hollow core.

Part of the payback for the martyr is receiving the praise of others. Everyone notices the martyr, and this makes him or her happy to some extent. However, the person receives not just attention, but admiration as well. This can be one of the most seductive things of all with which to deal. When people project all of their goodness onto us and put us on a pedestal, it can be very heady stuff indeed. For a while, we may actually feel good about ourselves. However, eventually the bubble bursts and our old feelings of inferiority return. Thus is set up the potential for an addiction to praise which is just as destructive as an addiction to alcohol or drugs.

There is, as with all of these dysfunctional patterns, something of value here. At least the martyr is not, on the surface, fixated on herself. She seems to care about the needs of others as well as herself. Of course, we might quibble about whether or not it is genuine help or just co-dependence that keeps the helper feeling inferior. On one level, the martyr may end up doing a lot of good in the world. The arrogant person or the greedy person could stand just a little bit of their energy. It might balance them out somewhat.

Any fear-based, shame-based, false personality pattern will have the same effect on us eventually. We simply cannot fill up that spiritual void within us with anything or any label or any person. Playing the role of the martyr is one of those scenarios that seems close to doing so on the surface. After all, here is someone who is not doing just good things, but holy things. What could be wrong with that? What is wrong with that approach is that it is an attempt to look for happiness outside of oneself, through the reactions of others. Real healing, on the other hand, only comes from one place: from deep inside the human soul.

7.Self Destruction – While all of the survival personalities are, at root, self destructive, most do not appear to be that way on the surface. With this particular pattern, the self-destructiveness is out there for all to see.

These are the individuals who always live on the edge of life. They may consume too much alcohol and food, or take drugs, or drive too fast, or practice unsafe sex, or get in fights, or get involved with a criminal element, and are usually in the habit of taking foolish risks most of the time. Any one of these things would not necessarily be cause for panic, but it is the consistent pattern of such behavior that is the problem. It is almost as if they have a script that says, "I will die young." They are a time bomb waiting to detonate. Everyone can see it. But few understand what it is all about and no one seems to be able to do anything about it. The sad part is that their self-fulfilling prophecy usually does come true. They usually do not live very long.

What is the self-destructive personality pattern, arguably the rarest pattern, really all about? For one thing, these individuals get attention. It may be negative attention, but it is attention nevertheless. It is a niche in the family and in society. The individual may be labeled the black sheep of the family, the *enfant terrible* of society, but at least everyone knows who they are. People may be afraid of them, but they have a very clear identity. Family members are concerned about them and will frequently cover for them, make excuses for them, and bail them out of trouble.

Another thing that arises from this pattern is lots of excitement. Studies have indicated that people can, eventually, become addicted to crisis. The same could be said about excitement. Like a cocaine addict who is bored even by the birth of a baby, the self-destructive person gets addicted to the adrenaline-pumping life of living dangerously. Ordinary life is seen as too flat, too boring, too run-of-the-mill.

In addition, this person achieves the illusion of a kind of immortality or at least a sense of being on the side of the gods. In their own way, they develop a kind of pseudo-spirituality. They invoke God's name a lot, often in vain, but sometimes with gratitude as they say, "Thank God", after having cheated the jaws of death once more. The attitude seems to be, "If God or the angels or whomever saved me from this near disaster, I must not be so bad after all. Somebody 'up there' loves me."

The self-destructive person is always putting himself (and God's providence) to the test. Because self-destructive people feel so empty inside, they try to fill up their void by patching it up with what is supposedly divine intervention. Like the cat who has nine lives, they seem to get away with things that would sink most of us. Eventually, however, they tempt the fates one time too often. It is only a matter of time before the liver breaks down, or AIDS is contracted, or they get severely injured in a fight, or their speeding car is in an accident, or they get into trouble with the law.

What this person is obliquely acknowledging is that life the way most people live it leaves a lot to be desired. On one level, of course, that assessment is correct. Many people do in fact lead lives of quiet desperation, in a low-grade depression. They never enjoy life. In fact, many people do not know what joy even is. At least the person who lives life on the edge challenges us to look for excitement in life. Where this person goes wrong, of course, is that they never attain joy either. What they attain is pleasure, thrills, kicks. In the end, however, there is no amount of pleasure, thrills, or kicks, that can satisfy the longings of the human heart.

This idea of a survival personality seems to answer a lot of questions for people. It helps to explain the origins of many of our character defects and personality problems. To be a human being is to have a survival personality, by whatever name we call it. In fact, we may even find ourselves having *more than* one survival personality pattern. This is perfectly understandable. This just means that we have made a lateral move and tried other popular ways of living our lives. The only people who do not have a survival personality are very little children, people with certain mental conditions like Downs syndrome, and mystics. All the rest of us need a spiritual journey back to our center because we are so out of touch with our inner magnificence.

Before we consciously begin an inner journey, though, we usually look outside ourselves for the answers. Traditionally, human beings have looked for happiness through money, sex, and power. Our next chapter will explore this important area that most of us know so well. For, it is not until we have looked there in depth, and come up empty, that we are ready to look deeper within.

II. Living an
Inauthentic Life

CHAPTER FOUR

Money, Sex, and Power

Every religious system tries, in its own way, to deal with the role of money, sex, and power on the spiritual path. Some approaches try to show how a person can use the energies without becoming used *by* them. Other approaches advocate "sublimating" the energies, transmitting the energies into lives of service. Taking vows of poverty, chastity, and obedience represents such a system. The idea is to "sublimate" the drives for money (through poverty), sex (through chastity), and power (through obedience).

The fact that all religious systems take these drives so seriously is testimony to their enduring power. Every human being who has ever walked the face of planet earth has had to find a way to come to terms with them.

The consensus seems to be that – if we handle the energies well – they need not be a problem on the spiritual path. While this is literally true, there seems to be agreement on the fact that very few of us succeed in mastering these energies. And, when that happens, we can get derailed from our journey back to divine consciousness. (see Figure 7)

Money, Sex, & Power

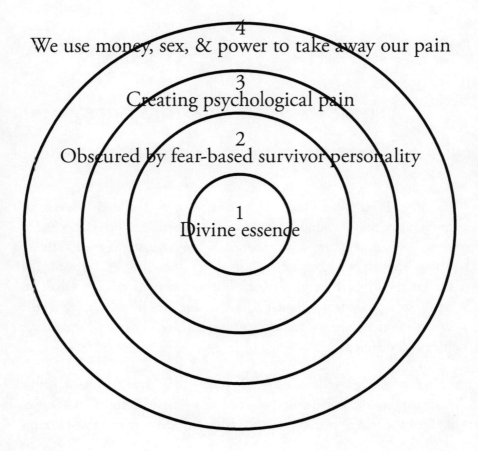

Figure Seven

Because money, sex, and power are such huge realities for us to handle, we must deal with them in this book about the psychological steps involved in spiritual growth. We could start by examining any of these drives, but let us begin by taking a look at money.

The Money Game

What is money? In its most literal sense, it is pieces of paper and coins that are used to represent the gold that was stored in a vault somewhere by the government. But the government no longer makes the claim that it has the precious metal to back up the paper or the coins. What it now represents is the promise of a changing government that it is somehow "good" for the paper. Today, it is even less about paper and coin and more about numbers in a computer. If the computers all break down, does that now mean that all of our money disappears?

Money is a total abstraction. It has no real permanence or independent existence. But, you counter, even though it is an abstraction, it enables us to do things here on this earth. That is true. As a game, it is fine. There is nothing wrong with the game at all. The only difficulty is when we make the money game our god, the only game in town. When we think that money is all that we need, when it acquires a disproportionate importance in our lives, then our lives revolve around it and suffering begins.

The funny thing about money (or material possessions of any type) is that it is all about much deeper issues. It is more about security, options, freedom, power, self-worth, and choices. The money game is the battleground for all sorts of other issues.

The money game can be a great way to learn many lessons in life. In addition, the point needs to be made that there is nothing intrinsically wrong with money. As the coin of the realm, it can enable us to provide a good standard of living for ourselves and our families. If it helps us have more freedom and more choices, that has to be good for the soul. A lot of New Age types do not understand this point at all. They seem to think that money is evil and, as a result, seldom seem to have enough of it. If your consciousness secretly abhors something, you will find ways to avoid it. So some people have the opposite problem: they undervalue money.

Most people in our Western culture, however, clearly go the other way. They overvalue what money can do for them. Such individuals will find out for themselves soon enough that money promises more than it can deliver. However, every step to maturity is by definition immature. We need to find out for ourselves what works for us and what does not work. That is why I never condemn anyone who is in the process of making what looks to me like a big mistake. I have compassion for them because they are, perhaps unwittingly, choosing a hard life for themselves; at the very least, they are about to learn a painful lesson for themselves.

It usually takes a long, long time to play this money game to its final conclusion. In fact, the temptation to place more importance on money and everything it represents usually increases with age. I remember an old priest telling me years ago that when he was a young priest, the toughest vow for him was chastity. When we are young, we are biologically programmed to place a high premium on the body with its demands, drives, and instincts. Later in his middle years, obedience was the vow that gave him the most trouble. Exerting his personal power was the most important thing to him. In his senior years he was surprised to find that the vow of poverty was the toughest thing for him to handle. While his physical drives had waned, and while his personality had mellowed, his need for material security was stronger than ever.

Whether we find out the limitations of money when we are young or when we are older, part of the spiritual path is coming to the realization that there is only so much that things can offer us. You can't hurry this process along. It is natural and it is organic. So if you are still living for money, perhaps you need to play this drama out to its end game. How long will this take? It will take as long as it takes.

The Sex Game

Just as there is nothing inherently wrong with money, there is nothing inherently wrong with sex, either. Or, putting this more positively, both money and sex can be a part of a person's spiritual path. It is just that they can never be a *substitute* for a spiritual path.

A distinction needs to be made here at the very beginning. Sexuality is not the same thing as sex. And sex is not the same thing as genitality. Let us throw one more distinction into the mix: sensuality is not the same thing as sexuality.

Sexuality has to do with our maleness and our femaleness. This is part of our hard wiring. We cannot not be sexual beings. Everywhere we go, whatever we do, we do as sexual creatures. Sex, on the other hand, is the act of touching and being touched for the sake of erotic pleasures. Genitality refers to the use of the sex organs for the same purpose, usually involving some form of intercourse. Sensuality has to do with the pleasure that the use of the five senses can bring us.

The denial of our sexual hard wiring is where, I think, the "Heaven's Gate" community went way off track. That was the UFO group who committed mass suicide in 1997. Implicit in their teaching is the assumption that, as we grow spiritually, we outgrow our maleness and femaleness. When you look into their teachings, a central tenet seems to be that we must progress to "the level above human." This phrase was used over and over again in their indoctrination of new members.

In a sense, this teaching is correct, but it is also horribly off the mark. In what sense is it correct? We are here to learn lessons, to progress, to raise our consciousness, to become fully aware of and aligned with our spiritual nature. So far so good. However, the crucial mistake that is made here is that the insinuation seems to be that the way to do this is to discount the role of the body on the spiritual path and to disparage, in a special way, the role of sexuality here on the earth.

There were many intelligent and educated members of the Heaven's Gate community (as well as some who were not so intelligent or educated). How could people buy into the distortion? As a student of philosophy, we had a professor who helped us understand why heresies are so attractive. It is because they are all partially true. He used to say, in debunking whatever philosopher did not agree with Catholic thought, "Please remember that there is a grain of truth to this teaching." He explained that the word "heresy" comes from the Greek and means "partial". So his point was that every heresy is true, but only partially true, and it is this fact that makes it a heresy.

The "Heaven's Gate" people were not as unusual as a lot of pundits have tried to make them out to be. Some of the parallels with Catholic monastic groups are almost scary. Both groups live in community, pool their resources, own no private property, wear common clothing, cut their hair short, practice celibacy, obey their religious superior, fast, meditate, and long for heaven. The monastic community, however, has produced intellectual and spiritual greats like Theresa of Avila and Thomas Merton. The "Heaven's Gate" community left little of value behind them, in words or deeds, as they committed mass suicide and headed off to join the Hale Bopp comet as it whisked through the heavens.

Their tragic flaw was, in my opinion, that they believed that we should abandon the body and the earth, instead of finding the spiritual core *in* the body and in the earth. They believed, for example, in advocating castration for the men in the community, since the body is only "the vehicle" for the spirit. It never seems to have occurred to them that the body itself could be holy. Rather than seeing the body as "charged with the grandeur of God", as poet Gerard Manley Hopkins put it, the body was seen as an obstacle to be overcome on the road to glory.

Once again, there is a grain of truth here. The drives of the body do need to be harnessed and channeled and coordinated and sublimated to a higher level. However, the goal is not to run away from the body. Instead, we are to discover the eminent worthwhileness of the body and even to investigate the possibility of using the body as a pathway to spiritual consciousness.

In the East, there is much more of a tradition for this than in the West. The East has, for example, yoga, elaborate teachings on diet, and Tantra, the practice of using sex consciously as a pathway to spiritual illumination. There will be an explanation of Tantra in the chapter on anger and sexuality.

I have searched the Western spiritual tradition high and low, and have found very little interest in the body at all. Sure, there are the dietary laws of Judaism, the fasting of Islam, and vestiges of fasting in Christianity. As far as sacred sex goes, however, there is very little consciousness around this possibility. Certain elements within Judaism advocate sexual relations on the Sabbath, and Christians have the sacrament of matrimony, but that is about it. The idea of sex as a form of meditation, as is the case with Tantra, is a concept that seems to have never occurred to us in the West.

Perhaps it is a bit premature in the book to be writing about sacred sex. We can address that crucial topic later on. Here we need to back up a few steps and deal with the fact that, for many if not most people, sexuality and sex are identical, and there is nothing sacred about any of it. Certainly that is the thinking of Madison Avenue and all of the other hidden persuaders of our culture. Sex, for them, is about pleasure, pure and simple.

Because sex is so debased in our society, dealing with it seems to most to have nothing at all to do with the spiritual journey. In fact, it is often seen as the opposite of spirituality or, at best, on parallel tracks that will never converge in a million years. As such, it becomes a kind of substitute for spirituality. And, as such, it will never ever become that.

Remember what my old philosophy teacher said about there being a grain of truth in all sorts of different points of view? Well, this is another case in point. For some people, in fact, sexual experiences can be moments that put them in touch with the flow of life to some extent. These experiences can be epiphanies, moments of breakthrough to higher truths and levels of consciousness. However, and this is the crucial point, this breakthrough will be very unlikely to happen if one is using the other person as an object and the total point of the experience is limited to release of tension or the experience of pleasure.

Is it fair to say that this is the way most people look upon sexual experiences? I think so, especially for the young who have not yet had the chance to find out for themselves that sex can never be a *substitute* for consciousness of our divinity.

The sexual hand of cards, just like the money hand, needs to be played out before people are ready to look elsewhere. What young person in the history of the world has ever listened to their elders when it comes to sex? In fact, each generation seems to feel as if it has *invented* sex! No, people will go down this alley for as many years or decades as it takes them before they are ready to even consider the possibility that there might be some other place to look for happiness.

The Power Game

Could that place to look be power? Once again, a lot of people tend to think so. Even those who practice celibacy and work for very little money are often seduced by this dragon. What is wrong with power? As is the case with money and sex, absolutely nothing. It is the *abuse* of power that is the problem. The word "abuse" comes from the Latin words *ab usare*, which means to use something in a way it is not meant to be used.

Every one is born with personal power. It is part of our hard wiring. We are all meant to make our mark, to exert our influence, to make a difference. As someone who worked for years as a therapist, I constantly reminded people that they have personal power, that they can always choose, that they have a right to be themselves. Those reminders were necessary because so many people give their personal power away. Because they have a need to be liked, or because they are afraid of getting some people upset, some people roll over, cave in, and sell themselves out for the modern equivalent of thirty pieces of silver.

Even though it may look as if some people are giving away their personal power, is not everyone actually engaged in the game of power? Remember back when we spoke about the survival personality. There it was noted that even the two types that appear to be self-effacing, the martyr and the self-deprecating person, are actually trying to manipulate reality to protect themselves.

The psychologist who wrote the most about power was Alfred Adler. Adler had been a disciple of Freud, who pointed to the belief that libido (meaning the sex drive), was the main motivator for people. Adler saw it somewhat differently. He believed that we humans do what we do in order to acquire personal and institutional power, thereby enabling us to survive and win over others.

The first time I heard this theory, it did not seem very convincing to me. But, as I have experienced life, it has made more and more sense to me. The aggressive person and the passive-aggressive, are they not two sides of the same coin? Aren't we all trying to protect ourselves, to survive, and to get our piece of the pie?

If we believe that power is wrong or even evil, then we will perhaps resist the implications of this theory. There are some people who think that competition is inherently bad, unspiritual, a kind of regressive, macho, Neanderthal activity. However, look at it this way. All of life is in a competition to survive. Human life itself begins with millions of sperm cells competing with one another to fertilize an egg. The winner helps to initiate a new life.

Competition is not inherently bad and power is not inherently abusive. It is only their misuse that is a problem. Consider the ability of personal power to make this a better world in which to live. Martin Luther King was a person who had enormous personal power and influence. He used his power, not for the aggrandizement of self, but for the empowerment of African Americans, an empowerment that was a direct benefit to all society.

Some other names of people with an acute sense of their personal power that come to mind are Jesus, Mahatma Gandhi, Malcolm X, Martin Luther, Mother Theresa, and Rosa Parks. These individuals went deep into the well of their personal being and brought forth vision and personal initiative that has changed the world. Through the force of their vision, which touched a chord in the psyche of humanity, they literally helped to change the world.

This sort of personal power is in each one of us. It is part of our hard wiring. When it is harnessed to a strong will, we can move mountains.

Such personal power should, perhaps, be referred to as transpersonal power. For it is not about the ego, especially not distorted manifestations of the ego like narcissism and grandiosity. No, it is about owning the fact that we are part of a whole. When we can overcome our fears and let the transpersonal Truth speak through us, there is no telling what we might be able to accomplish with our lives.

Let me reiterate this a second time: there is nothing grandiose about such consciousness. It is the simple realization that we are free and spiritual, therefore powerful beyond our imaginations.

Believing this and feeling this very strongly, it distresses me greatly when I see someone playing the role of the victim. You hear people say, for example, "I don't have any choice in the matter." I must confess that I used to think that way myself a lot. A friend of mine straightened me out when he told me, "Tom, you always have a choice. You might have to pay something as a result of your choice. But you always have options." It is amazing what these simple words did for me. Rather than feeling backed into a corner, without choices, playing the victim,

I experienced the reality of my personal power. I listened to my heart and learned how to act on what I heard from within. The result of this shift in my thinking was that I felt the onerous but liberating truth that I could do anything with my life that I chose to do with it. What this led to was a lifting of low-level depression, a surge in creativity, and a strengthening of my immune system. Today I feel incredibly healthy and energized and grateful and free. This result can be experienced by you, too, as you return to the center of your being and find therein the storehouse of your inner treasure.

Besides personal power, there is also corporate or institutional power. This kind of power comes as a result of your association with a group that has a lot of clout. The corporation or institution is a force in itself. It gets people's attention, and must be dealt with, because it wields either monetary or moral influence.

This sort of power can be used either constructively or destructively. When it is used constructively, the world can be changed for the better. As an example, let us consider Pope John Paul II. He held the office of head of millions of Catholics. The office is unlike that of any other political leader. Since the office makes claims to divine origin and inspiration, it is charged with people's projections. The Pope, whoever he might be, is a walking archetype. He embodies the archetype of the Divine King. Whoever holds the office has incredible influence on people, even if the person holding the office lacks charisma, intelligence, or moral fiber. But when an individual possesses all of these qualities, as Pope John Paul II does, he can wield institutional power in a way that reshapes the globe.

Pope John Paul II generally is considered to be a disappointment to leaders of church reform. In fact, he has tried to stop much reform and actually reverse momentum. However, on the world stage, he is a much different figure. He has used all of his abilities, including his ability as a trained actor, to help deconstruct the Soviet empire. When one reads the memoirs of ex-CIA chief William Casey as well as others who were instrumental in toppling the hegemony of the Soviet bloc, Pope

John Paul II is shown to be one of the major behind-the-scenes players in dismantling the Soviet empire. All of this without a standing army (except for the ax-wielding Swiss Guard), without a sophisticated media office, and without the ability to levy taxes. It is institutional power in its best possible expression.

Of course, every day we see the abuses of institutional power. One thinks immediately of large corporations which think nothing of disrupting people's lives by massive layoffs and factory closings. These actions are undertaken with only one motive being considered: corporate profits. What is particularly galling is that many of these factories are making a good profit. But, with corporate acquisitions and mergers, whole sectors may be cast aside because somebody thinks that they can make a cheaper widget somewhere else. The widget costs less because the company has found someone who will work for a lesser salary.

This sort of abuse of corporate power is what gives power a bad name in some circles. But let us be clear that the problem is always in the *abuse* of power and not in the nature of power itself. In itself, power is neither good nor bad. It just is. What we do with the power, whether we use it to build up or to tear down, is entirely our choice.

Money, sex, and power are incredible powerful in their own right. They represent inherent potentialities within each one of us. Adding to their allure is the fact that our Western culture genuinely seems to believe that they hold the key to human happiness. Driven by our inner urges, spurred on by the distorted values of society, it is easy and almost inevitable that we make excessive investments in these three energies in our pursuit of happiness. What human being does not carry some scars as a result of such an overinvestment?

In the end, we will find that, with the discovery of the divine energies within, we are gifted with more pleasure and power than we ever thought possible. But, before we come to that realization, we usually have to go down a lot of dead-end streets.

The mistakes that we make along the way produce a lot of psychic pain. Before we find what we are really looking for, we often look for ways to deaden the pain that is crippling us. That is where addiction enters the picture. Our next chapter will explore why it is that some form of substance abuse is often a part of the inner journey for so many of us.

CHAPTER FIVE
Addiction

When we are living lives that are "off center", we experience pain. We are like wobbly wheels, somehow rolling along, but out of synch, unbalanced, paying a heavy price for everything that we do. Living out of our fear-based survival personality causes distress to ourselves and our loved ones.

What we need, of course, is a spiritual wheel alignment. We ultimately need to find our center and to become aligned to it. In the short term, not realizing what we ultimately need, we go for the quick fix. We seek something, anything, that will take away the pain that our soul feels. That is where substance abuse and addiction come into the picture. We think that taking alcohol or drugs, or engaging in some activity like gambling or acting-out sexually, will relieve us of our pain.

To some extent, these behaviors do seem to work, at least in the beginning. People usually do what they think will ultimately be in their best self-interest. Mind-altering substances and mind-altering behaviors are so popular because they give an immediate, albeit short lived, payback to us. (see Figure 8)

Addiction

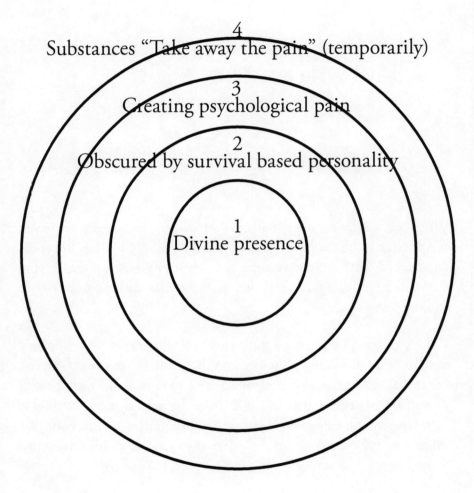

Figure Eight

Bill W., one of the founders of Alcoholics Anonymous, speaks about his first experience with alcohol in almost mystical terms. He felt elated that the alcohol made him feel less self conscious, less anxious, more confident, more connected with the other people in the room. Those are all beautiful benefits. Spiritual teachers say that spirituality is supposed to do the same thing for us.

If alcohol can do that for someone, then imagine what some of the designer drugs can deliver. The power of heroin is legendary. Its effect can be so immediate and pleasurable that someone can become psychologically "hooked" after taking it only one time. There is, however, nothing as dangerous as cocaine. It is dangerous because it produces a feeling like no other feeling. I remember one person telling me that she only tried cocaine one time. She never tried it again, not because it produced any adverse effects, but it provided her the most pleasurable experience of her life. She said something that many users of cocaine say: "It was better than sex." Other cocaine users have told me that it gave them incredible self-confidence. They felt that there was nothing in the whole world that they could not do. Imagine the allure that this kind of thinking has for someone who has been ineffective at whatever they have tried in life.

While there are physical aspects to addiction, to be sure, there are also these psychological or spiritual aspects as well. An alcoholic may indeed have more physical susceptibility to alcohol, but that does not preclude the psychological and spiritual payoffs as being a big part of the disease as well. While we continue to do research on how medicine can contribute to the cure of alcoholism, the experience seems to be that there are psychological and social and spiritual aspects to alcoholism as well.

Sometimes, of course, the effect of the substance or behavior does not sound anything like the quasi-mystical experience that Bill W. experienced. It sounds, rather, like the effect that taking anesthesia might have on a person. An example from television that many people can relate to is the effect that alcohol has on Andy Sipowicz of *NYPD*

Blue. There is no quasi-mystical experience for Andy. Instead, this hurting individual is able to find relief from his inner demons by drinking himself into oblivion. I can still remember the episode when Andy finds out that his son Andy Jr., a police officer like him, has been killed in the line of duty. Andy, who has been attending AA meetings until this time, is overwhelmed by grief. He heads to the local tavern and tells the bartender, "Line 'em up." The bartender pours three shots of whiskey at once in front of him. Andy belts them down in three gulps. There is no pretense of social drinking here. And there certainly is nothing about his drinking that seems to mimic a spiritual experience for him. There is only the washing away of his pain through the effects of the alcohol.

Even though it may look like Andy is not doing anything spiritual here, I still see some parallels with spiritual consciousness. For is not spiritual consciousness supposed to give one a sense of inner peace and a feeling of being connected with all things? Of course it is. One might say that what Andy is doing is not something spiritual. Fair enough. But is he not *looking for* ultimately what the mystic has? What person lost in the subculture of addiction would not trade it all in a minute if they could be promised that there was something *better* as an alternative?

This is what the genius of AA is based upon. Not a shaming or a condemning of people; not the injunction to conquer their problems with old-fashioned willpower; but the realization that spiritual consciousness is a lot more healthy and satisfying and even more pleasurable than artificial highs. It involves communicating to people that alcohol, drugs, gambling, etc. produce an altered state of consciousness that *mimics* true spiritual awareness, but is not the real thing. Most importantly, the program gives people a way to *experience* the reservoirs of spirituality that lie deeply buried within them. The idea is that, when they drink deeply from these springs of living water, they will not need the substitutes that they have been relying upon until then.

The connection between artificial highs and spiritual experience has always been recognized through the ages. For example, the ancient

Greeks had their Dionysian rites, which were designed to lead people to a mystical sense of death and rebirth of the ego. Dionysius was, of course, the god of wine and drunkenness. But what some people overlook is that Dionysius was also the god of ecstasy. The word "ecstasy" comes from the Greek and means literally "to stand outside of oneself." Ecstasy is one of the hallmarks of mystical experience. Thus, consciously or unconsciously, the Greeks linked up an altered state of consciousness with the altered state of ecstasy. Does anyone seriously think it is just a coincidence that one of the most popular drugs among young people today is called "ecstasy"? Psychologist Carl Jung was prophetic when he said that the phenomenon of widespread use of alcohol and drugs was a modern day equivalent of "the thirst for wholeness." He said, more specifically, that spirits (liquor) was an ineffective substitute for "spiritus" (the latin word for spirit).

This ancient connection of artificially induced altered states of consciousness with mystical states of consciousness even has a parallel with some religious practice. For example, some form of mind-altering drugs has been used for thousands of years in many of the rituals of the great religions of the world, including the Roman Catholic Mass.

Wine is used – on the esoteric level – as a symbol of the need to not be fixated on the ego level (the survival personality). The goal is to become, as it were, "intoxicated" with God. The point of using the wine is not, of course, to become literally intoxicated. The same could be said for the use of mind-altering drugs in any religious service. The wine, or the drugs, point to an altered state of consciousness that mimics higher states of awareness. That higher state of consciousness would include a loss of self-consciousness, a letting go of ego control, creativity, and a sense of being a part of a reality greater than oneself.

The Twelve Step movement itself even had some confusing crossover experiences in its beginnings. For example, it is a "family secret" of the Twelve Step community that Bill W. went through a period of experimentation with LSD (as recounted at length in *Pass It On*). Of course, this attempt at pharmaceutical mysticism never got much support from the AA community, and Bill W. eventually jettisoned the practice, but the indisputable facts of the matter are that the founder of AA himself sensed that the mystic and the addict are essentially looking for the same thing.

The trick, of course, is to see the substance as a metaphor and not get hooked into a literal acting out with the substance or behavior in question. So, while it is healthy to be "intoxicated with God," as many mystics have been accused of being, it is not healthy to get stuck on being literally intoxicated.

When Bill W., one of the founders of Alcoholics Anonymous, had only his intuition to guide him, he was fortunate enough to come upon Swiss psychologist Dr. Carl G. Jung. Jung impressed upon Bill W. that spiritual consciousness is the only thing that can ultimately quench the thirst of an alcoholic or the craving of any addict.

Dr. Jung pointed out that the word for alcohol in Latin is *spiritus,* the same word that also refers to the spiritual principle within human beings. Jung further noted that wanting to "get high" is a term that has spiritual parallels. Spiritual searchers have always used terms like heightened consciousness, mountaintop experiences, and religious peak experiences. Addicts may have thought that they knew how to get high. With the discovery of their spiritual resources, however, they have finally come upon the real goal of their search.

It is amazing how many spiritual searchers have had some experience of pharmaceutical mysticism as part of their path. At least in the early days of development of LSD, research and experimentation with LSD were legal. Some had mystical experience as a result of that research. For a fascinating account of this, read *The Varieties of Psychedelic Experience*[5] by Robert Masters and Jean Houston. When people began to hear about these effects back in the late 60's, and after the research had been outlawed by the government, many continued to experiment illegally on their own. As we all know, this sometimes led to "bad trips". But I am still amazed by how many people still report that they had consciousness changing experiences with LSD or with marijuana or other mind-altering drugs. When I hear these stories, the old religious phrase comes to mind, "God works in strange ways."

No spiritually mature person would ever say that alcohol and drugs are the final destination. However, many, if truth be told, have had some experiences of these things as part of their journeys. The trick, once again, is to look beyond the signpost to the true goal waiting for us on the other side.

There is nothing wrong with alcohol and drugs (many people would not be alive without prescription drugs). In fact, there are positive aspects to these things. It is just that drugs and alcohol can never be a *substitute* for the real deal.

Food, Sex and Gambling

Beside drugs and alcohol, there are other substances and behaviors that purport to take away the pain. In our culture, in particular, we seem to be particularly fond of food, sex, and gambling. Obviously, the misuse of food, sex, and gambling bring untold suffering to millions of people. However, let us say here, for the record, that food and sex are two of the greatest blessings in life. Even gambling is not inherently evil. It is the misuse of these things that is the problem. Part of that misuse - at least unconsciously - is to use them to try to fill up a spiritual void. Let us briefly examine food, sex, and gambling and ask ourselves what are the psychological issues involved in their use and in their abuse.

Food

What does food do for us? Three things: 1) it fills us up; 2) it nourishes us; and 3) it provides us pleasure. I would submit that Higher Power does all three of the above, only better. To bolster the claim, I would only suggest a reading of the Hebrew scriptures, especially the Psalms. The above three metaphors are employed constantly. God (Higher Power) fills up the hunger of the human heart. Higher Power nourishes our souls. And living in union with the Higher Power is the equivalent of living in the land of milk and honey. Perhaps this is one of the reasons that food plays such a big role in Jewish culture. Contact with God was often put in terms of culinary references. Even the most famous Jewish person of all time, Jesus of Nazareth, used bread and wine to communicate with his followers.

Of course, there are other issues concerning food besides spiritual nourishment. Food can be used as a palliative to try to avoid the pains of life. The subsequent additional weight that one then gains is then unconsciously perceived as a type of insulation, a form of padding. The pounds serve to produce the illusion of a protective coating for the soul.

Another aspect of food abuse is that weight problems are often found in cases of persons who were sexually abused as children. This is not to imply that every person with a weight problem is a sexual abuse survivor. But it is to imply that at least my colleagues and I (with hundreds of years of experience between us) have seldom seen a sexually abused person who did not have food and/or weight issues. Sometimes the person may tend towards obesity; sometimes the presenting problem will be anorexia nervosa or bulimia. But the common denominator usually seems to be the issue of food.

While we should avoid overly simplifying, there do often seem to be these spiritual dimensions to food. Even the sexually abused person who develops a problem with food is dealing with a spiritual issue. A person's soul has been violated. A trusting individual has been betrayed. Innocence has been lost. What could be more of a spiritual issue than that?

Besides filling us up, food nourishes us. As human beings we simply cannot live without it. Can we not say the same thing about contact with our true self and with Higher Power? Of course. The person who misuses food, however, thinks that earthly food is the source of the nourishment. That is the tragedy. The food alone can never do it. We can eat tons of it and still be unhappy. Or we can study food scientifically, and eat only "health foods", and end up just as spiritually hungry.

There are many ways of attaining "I am" consciousness about what Jesus and the Buddha spoke. However, consuming gross amounts of food is not one of them. That is where the wisdom of fasting enters the picture. The original idea of fasting had nothing to do with masochism or body hatred. It had to do with the truth that overindulgence with food bloats the human spirit. Fasting was seen as a way of ultimately feeding the soul by helping it to attain "I am" consciousness.

When Jesus says, "I am the Bread of Life", he is not saying that he, Jesus, is the only answer. But what he is saying is that the "I am" consciousness is the only thing that can ultimately satisfy the hungers of the human heart.

The mix-up with the food addict is the same mix-up that the drug and alcohol abuser makes. It is to confuse the means with the end, the medium with the message, the metaphor with the reality. Clearly, no amount of food (a lot or a little) and no sensual pleasure can ever, by themselves, give a person the "I am" consciousness. But the filling up and the pleasure mimic what can only come from a shift in awareness.

What about the pleasure that food brings us? Once again, there is nothing wrong with pleasure. Only a sick, repressed soul would think that there is. The error comes in thinking that the pleasure that food brings is the greatest pleasure in life. While the delights of food are absolutely wonderful, they do not and cannot produce joy. They produce pleasure, but the pleasure is fleeting. Eating more food can only bring us more pleasure, not more joy. However, if one tastes the ultimately satisfying and pleasurable experience of being in contact with Higher Power, then the pleasures of food are put in their place. They have a place, to be sure, but they are now in a supplementary role to the real bread of life found within us all.

Sex

We have introduced the role of sex in life in the last chapter and chapter thirteen of this book deals with the role of sex on the spiritual path, but let us speak about the addictive aspects of sex at this point. Sex brings us at least four things: 1) pleasure; 2) a sense of union with another person; 3) the total release of orgasm; and 4) sometimes, participation in the creative process of life by parenting a new life.

The pleasure of sex is similar to the pleasure of food. As great as it is, it is not as great as the pleasure that one feels when one is in contact with the divine. Sexuality and spirituality, are not, however mutually opposed at all. One's sexuality can lead to a spiritual experience and reflect one's spiritual truth. It is precisely because sexuality and spirituality are so intertwined that it is easy to mistake the one for the other. That is the potential difficulty here: thinking that sex can ever *substitute* for spirituality.

It is easy to see how we so often can make this mistake. After all, if sex contains elements of pleasure, union, surrender, and creativity, does not this list of qualities reflect our spiritual dimension? It certainly does. However, while sex may be the path, the means, the metaphor, it is not in itself the answer. By the way, celibacy was originally recommended as *a* path (not *the* path) for some spiritual journeyers precisely because sex was seen to be so good and so powerful. Because of its goodness and power, it was easy to think that sex was *itself* the answer. Celibacy was presented as *a* valid path, not a superior one. The important thing was to attain union with God. Whether or not one used sex as part of one's path was a matter of personal choice. Twisted ideas concerning sexuality and spirituality arose later from twisted minds.

The surrender aspect of sex is one of its most powerful parts. Orgasm is probably the closest that the average person on the street ever gets to an act of surrender. It may only last for a short period, but the person feels connected, part of something beyond his own puny ego, not in control, able to let go. All spiritual teachers speak about union with the divine producing many of these same experiences. Of course, once again, the danger is to think that sex by itself is the ultimate human experience. While sex is certainly wonderful in itself, it points to union with the divine, perhaps the only thing in life that is better than sex.

Gambling

Is there anything spiritual - on an unconscious level - about the path of the gambler? I think that there is. When a person has risked everything, or at least a lot, this has a way of focusing the mind on something other than one's troubles. Imagine, for example, someone has just bet ten thousand dollars that he cannot afford to lose. He has bet it all on one turn of the wheel at a casino. If it stops on red, he wins. If it stops on black, he loses it all. During that time when the wheel is spinning, what do you think the gambler has on his mind? Is the gambler thinking that the grass has to be cut? Or that his arthritis has been acting up? No. Everything is focused on one proposition: winning or losing.

Much of Buddhist practice is aimed at what is called "one pointedness of mind." This is trying to discipline the "monkey mind" which jumps from thought to thought. Disciplining the mind this way is a very difficult thing to do. Monks spend years trying to master the practice. In their own unorthodox and ultimately destructive way, that is what the gambler succeeds in doing for a time. Of course, the one-pointedness-of-mind only lasts for as long as the wheel is spinning. When it stops, the "monkey mind" rushes in again. So do all of the worries and concerns about unpaid bills and bankrupt relationships. But it is possible to see how what the gambler does is a pale imitation of what the monk does: finds a way to focus on one thing only.

The gambler also experiences bio-chemical changes when the action is flowing. The adrenaline in the system produces a kind of a high that can become addictive itself. Without getting into the technicalities involved, the nervous system becomes dependent upon certain chemicals-in this case adrenaline-being in the bloodstream. When the action is flowing, so is the adrenaline. The body eventually becomes dependent upon the adrenaline. The action of gambling then makes the nervous system feel relieved.

Once again, there are parallels with spiritual experiences. In his research,[6] William Johnston, S.J., documents the bio-chemical changes that take place with monks who are in a state of meditation. Endorphins are produced which contribute to a mental state of wellbeing.

So where is the difference, then, between the gambler with the adrenaline and the monk with the endorphins? Are not each dependent upon a chemical produced by the body? They are. But there are a couple of differences between the two of them. First of all, the adrenaline will eventually break down the system of the body. Endorphins, on the other hand, are good for the body. Secondly, the adrenaline feeds into a fear-driven, almost manic state. The endorphins calm a person and make it easier to access the true self.

Finally, the gambler sometimes has a sense of being on the side of the gods. Observe gamblers. They are often very superstitious people. They carry charms and amulets with them. When they win, they will often say, "Thank God". They will sometimes, when they hit it big, give a donation to a church. They are not likely to give the donation to the American Cancer Society, but they have no problem buying a statue for their church or making a donation to their synagogue.

In a similar way, a person in the flow spiritually will often have an attitude of gratitude. Spiritual searchers often have a similar sense of being on the side of the gods. A fundamentalist might say, for example, "Thank you, Jesus." Even a non-religious (but spiritual) type might lift up their eyes and say, "Gratitude."

What is the difference, then, between the gambler and the spiritual searcher? In a nutshell, it is this: the gambler only feels blessed when winning; the spiritual type gives thanks "in season and out." The spiritual type grows to the point where all of life is seen as a blessing, even the challenges of life.

Conclusion

How long does it take to find the real truth that resides within us? It takes as long as it takes. It varies with the individual. In the spiritually bankrupt society in which we live, it often takes people a very long time to find their way. In the meantime, they continue to look to their society and to their religion. To many people, these sources do not seem to have the answer either. The pain continues and grows stronger. Addiction has become one of the signs of our times. It has become so because people are hurting a lot and they are desperately looking for answers, and certain substances and behaviors alter their consciousness for a while. In the end, as people break through to the reality behind the signposts, they will find that the answers all lie within. In the meantime, addiction continues to be on the rise all over the world.

To recap what we have so far seen about the journey to wholeness:

I. The ego (or self) is divine and, therefore, perfect.

II. The newborn soul initially reflects that divine perfection.

III. Some wounding to the soul, most typically by its primary caregivers, causes the child to lose its sense of innocence.

IV. There are many ways to be wounded, but they all result in the person feeling fear and a lack of safety.

V. This expulsion from the Garden of Eden results in a sense of alienation.

VI. Although we are already whole and perfect, very few of us feel that way.

VII. We then unconsciously create a survival personality to help us cope with the pain of life.

VIII. Over time, this survival personality creates its own pain.

IX. We look for relief - and happiness - in food, drugs, money, sex, and power.

X. When the pain persists, we often try substances and behaviors to alter our consciousness and "take away the pain."

When we survey the landscape of our lives, and take stock of the pain that we have caused ourselves and others, we frequently enter into a depression. This experience of going into the valley, of having a "dark night of the soul" (St John of the Cross), is very frequently part of the journey to wholeness for most people. In this next chapter, we will look at the different types of depression and try to understand how an experience that seems so negative and hopeless can be turned into a spiritual rebirth.

CHAPTER SIX

The Illness of Our Times

Not every depression is pathological, but some are. Not every depression has something to do with spiritual growth, but some do. This chapter will try to shed light on this widespread condition that we call depression. It will help us sort out the type of depression that should be fought with every once of strength that we have, from the type of depression that is an opportunity for growth.

If it is true that it is always the darkest just before the dawn, then depression must be a part of the dawning of our true selves. For nothing is more dark and more painful than depression.

It is difficult to imagine anything more painful than being locked into a deep depression. I have heard it said that this world can be divided into two groups of people: those who have back pain and those who do not. That is certainly true from my perspective. As will become evident later, the back pain syndrome is something I have known well. But I must say that there is something much more painful and devastating to deal with, and that is depression.

The big difference between back pain (and any other devastating physical ailment) and depression is that, with depression, the prognosis is much more uncertain. For that matter, so is its origin. These are the really scary aspects of depression: 1) you are never quite sure where it came from; 2) you are not sure when it will end; and 3) you are not entirely sure *if* it will ever end.

It is estimated that one out of three Americans will experience a bout of depression at some point in their lives. There is no question that this has become a serious problem, an American epidemic of sorts. However, lest we catastrophize here, there are some psychologists who feel that we have less depression today in our country than ever. The anger, fueled by alcohol, of brutal men who thought nothing of killing other human beings as well as millions of buffalo for "sport," must have been scary. In some respects, we have learned to manage our anger and depression a little better today. But two questions continue to present themselves: 1) what, if anything, can we do about depression; and 2) what does depression have to do with the spiritual journey and with finding our center?

In order to answer these questions, we need to understand that <u>there are three major types of depression</u>. One has virtually nothing to do with the spiritual journey; one is often a precursor to a spiritual breakthrough; and one is *all about* the spiritual path.

The type of depression that has virtually nothing to do with the spiritual path is a clinical depression. Let us define our terms here. What we are talking about is a depression with no apparent immediate cause, with severe symptoms, lasting six months to a year or more. This is a medical situation, healed primarily through medical means. In other words, medication needs to be part of the solution.

As I write these words, I am still surprised. For I was one of those believers in a wholistic point of view that never wanted to see medication as part of the solution. In most ways, I still embrace that philosophy. I believe firmly that we are comprised of body, mind and spirit. All three aspects need to be addressed and taken seriously.

Usually, the above argument is advanced by proponents of a wholistic philosophy as a way of insisting that the mind and the spirit must be a part of the healing equation. Fair enough. However, the argument cuts both ways. The body, too, must be taken seriously in order for healing to take place. While those in the wholistic movement do, indeed, take the role of the body seriously, they often stop at the doorstep of traditional medicine. While there is an openness to look at nutrition, exercise, rest, yoga, and various herbal and homeopathic approaches, once again there is often a closing of the mind when it comes to allopathic medicine. The reason that I know a bit about this mindset is that I have been working in the wholistic movement since 1980.

While continuing to espouse the necessity of a wholistic perspective in healing, I have also come to appreciate the important contribution that medication can make as well. Let me give a case study, based upon a true life experience, that helped me to reach this conclusion

Sandy's Story

Let us call her Sandy. She had been a client of mine for over ten years, dealing with an ever-deepening depression. Those were the days when I naively thought that spirituality could solve any problem. Sandy felt the same way. Her commitment to the spiritual path was beyond question. Far from being a dilettante, she practiced what she preached. With such an exceptional client, there was no doubt in my mind that she would never have a need for Prozac or any of the related meds that were beginning to become popular back in the 80's.

What initially appeared to be a minor and a manageable depression steadily escalated into something that was ominous and paralyzing. Not to worry. There were lots of wholistic remedies yet to be tried. Sandy was open to trying anything; anything except drugs. I completely concurred with her opinion.

Even though Sandy was already living a model wholistic lifestyle, she confidently and enthusiastically tried the following approaches, with my blessing.

- Massage

- Yoga

- Naturopathy

- Homeopathy

- Therapeutic Touch

- Meditation

- Jogging

- Weight resistance training

- Visualization

- Polarity

- Breathwork

- Rolfing

- Vegetarianism

- Muscle testing

- Psychodrama

- Journaling

- Dreamwork

After trying the above modalities, along with some that I undoubtedly cannot recall, Sandy did not get better at all. In fact, she got steadily worse. The change was not dramatic, but it was relentless and inexorable. After ten years of therapy, which is about eight or nine years longer than the counseling relationship I have with most of my clients, Sandy was no better than she had been at the start of counseling.

Finally, reluctantly, when all other avenues had been exhausted, Sandy was ready to at least consider the possibility of taking medication. However, first she had to overcome a psychological barrier. Until that time, Sandy had seen taking medication as a sign of failure. It was this last point that really stuck in her craw. Having recourse to medication was, in her way of thinking, implying that spirituality is not the answer to everything. It was saying, in effect, that the medical piece might just be part of the solution after all. This was the equivalent of heresy to a wholistic- minded, spiritual, natural soul.

After consulting a psychiatrist, Sandy began taking Zoloft, one of the new class of anti-depressants. It might be helpful here to explain in simple terms how this drug works.

Zoloft, along with Prozac and Paxil, represent the three most popular brands of anti-depressant medication today. Rather than giving people an artificial high, as an amphetamine might do, these drugs try to put people back on a level playing field with everyone else. They do this by helping the person to keep a substance called seratonin in the blood stream. Seratonin is naturally produced by the brain. It is associated with feelings of wellbeing. Research has shown that *no person* can experience normal feelings of wellbeing without an adequate level of seratonin.

Let us put this in practical terms that anyone can understand. Take any person that you admire. Perhaps you chose Mother Theresa, or Pope John Paul II, or Oprah Winfrey, or Nelson Mandela, Ralph Nader, or Hillary Clinton. Whomever. The point here is that if these people had seratonin removed from their bloodstream (procedures exist to enable this to happen), they would enter into a depression that they would be unable to overcome.

Seratonin is that important. So this new class of drugs simply enables the chronically depressed person to finally have the same amount of seratonin as everyone else. The research shows that, without the seratonin, you will be depressed. With the seratonin level restored to what it should be, there is every hope that you will be able to live a normal life. I was tempted to say, "live a normal life again." But that would not be an accurate statement in every instance. For some people have never lived a normal life.

When people start taking this new class of drugs called SSRI's (selective seratonin reuptake inhibitors), it normally takes three or four weeks before the medication begins to have the desired effect. In Sandy's case, within a few days one could see a difference already. It was as if her body was so depleted of seratonin that any change in her body was seen as dramatic. Within two weeks, the changes in her outlook were unbelievable. Within three weeks, it was miraculous. Within a couple of months, she was almost a different person. I hesitate to use the term "different person" because she was not acting in some way that resembled a manic state or borderline personality. No, she was very much herself, but now freer, calmer, more positive, more creative, less hostile, less irritable, and less self-deprecating.

This experience with Sandy changed my attitude toward taking medication for depression. In the limited cases of clinical depression, it is not only acceptable to use it, but usually imperative to do so.

A couple of points need to be made here about clinical depression and the use of SSRI's in dealing with it. First of all, there are various degrees of clinical depression. In other words, it is not a case of "Are you clinically depressed or not?" One has to ascertain the degree of clinical depression. In less severe cases of clinical depression, perhaps medication is not the answer. This will be a judgment call that should be made by a skilled psychiatrist. When people self-diagnose and ask their family physician for medication because they have read an article or two about it, they are rolling the dice with their own health.

The second caveat concerns the much touted SSRI's that we have spoken about earlier. While this class of medication has been, on balance, a Godsend to millions, people should be aware that there are sideeffects that have to be considered. For example, a very large percentage of people experience a lessening or total loss of their sex drive. This can have consequences for their relationship with their partner. In addition, too much of the medication in the system can cause the individual to manifest symptoms of mania or compulsiveness. I mention these things because it is difficult to have a spiritual state of consciousness when one is feeling "off–center."

Situational Depression

A situational depression is totally different from a clinical one. As the name implies, it is a depression that stems from a specific historical situation. In other words, you can point to something specific that triggered it. With Sandy's situation, on the other hand, there was absolutely nothing that anyone could find that explained its origin.

Examples of things that might cause a situational depression would be:

- the death of a loved one

- the breakup of a relationship

- the loss of a job

- an investment gone bad

- finishing a major project and then experiencing a letdown

- guilt as a result of behaving against one's moral code

- inability to pay one's bills

- being arrested and having one's reputation destroyed

- inability to control weight gain

- postpartum depression

- dealing with one's own aging process

- terminal illness of a child

This list is by no means exhaustive. There are countless occurrences in life that might be a catalyst to bring on a situational depression. Let us note here that sadness and mourning are not indicative of psychiatric illness. They are a natural and normal part of life. Furthermore, sadness and mourning are not the same thing as a depression. For example, a person may be in mourning for years over the loss of a loved one without being in a depression. No, depression is a specific illness with very specific criteria. Sometimes, an event of life might cause a depression, sometimes it will just cause a deep sadness.

The one thing that all of the examples cited have in common is that there is something concrete that we can point to that at least initiated the depression. Where we go from there, however, is a different story.

Some pains in life eventually heal themselves with the passage of time. We even have an expression for this: "Time heals all wounds." For example, the pain caused by a breakup of a relationship or the death of a loved one will often dissipate in time. Some situational depression can eventually turn into clinical depression. Whether situational or clinical, however, depression <u>can</u> lead us to greater self examination. The events that factored into depression can serve to kick off a deep questioning about one's life. If so, this can become part of what I call a spiritual depression.

Spiritual Depression

While there may be biochemical elements or situational elements present, a spiritual depression is fundamentally caused by a crisis of meaning. Questions concerning ultimate meaning are spiritual in nature, even though a person may not label them as such. Accordingly, some element of depression is frequently part of the spiritual odyssey of many people.

It takes discernment to be able to recognize a spiritual depression. Before arriving at the conclusion that this is what is being dealt with, other possibilities should be eliminated. I would begin by asking all of the usual questions about the depression that the client might have. How long have you been depressed? Is there any history of depression in your family? Et cetera. Let us say that, after duly investigating all possibilities, we rule out a clinical depression.

The next line of questioning would explore the possibility of a situational depression. Have there been any unusually traumatic events in your life lately? Tell me about the things that have been happening in your life and in the life of your family recently.

I realize that this section is approaching things from the vantage point of a typical therapist. I do this because it might be helpful for the client to understand how the different possibilities for depression are eliminated.

Let us say that, after having done this, we are left with two possibilities: 1) the client has been impacted in a very deep way by a situational depression; or 2) the client is depressed because of an existential void that has no answer to the question, "Is this all there is?" Either way, we may be in the presence of a spiritual depression. And, if that is the case, then the old principles of mental health do not apply.

The first principle that many therapists might espouse in a situation like this would be to try to alleviate the mental suffering. While this goal may be well intentioned, it is ill advised and counterproductive to the person's growth.

One of the ways that mental health professionals might need to alleviate suffering is through the use of medication. The last thing that an individual in such a situation needs is a dose of powerful, psychotropic, psychiatric drugs which numb the psyche. From what I understand, use of one of the SSRI's would not present a problem since they only work if the person is clinically depressed. The same goes for Saint John's Wort or other herbal remedies. I have tried Saint John's Wort and it did not do a thing for me. That is because I am not depressed. So the SSRI's or the herbal remedies are not the problem here. What would be a problem would be any medication whose main purpose is to anesthetize the patient.

Not only should we not try to anesthetize the patient, I think we should, if anything, turn up the heat a little. Let the individual experiencing the spiritual depression stew in their own juices for a while. This is not being cruel or manipulative. It is simply recognizing what every good midwife knows intuitively. In order for the birth to take place, there will have to be some pain involved. Pain is not the same thing as suffering. Suffering has to do with our interpretation of the situation. Suffering can be changed by a change in perspective, but pain is visceral, immediate, in no need of any interpretation.

The wise therapist will recognize this and bless the pain. As we are struggling to let go of the past and surrender to the present and the future, there will inevitably be some amount of pain. This pain can ultimately be creative and redemptive.

Spiritual depression, then, is something unique. It is not a clinical depression, nor is it a situational depression that may go away in time. It is inner pain at the service of the soul's emergence. (see Figure 9)

Depression

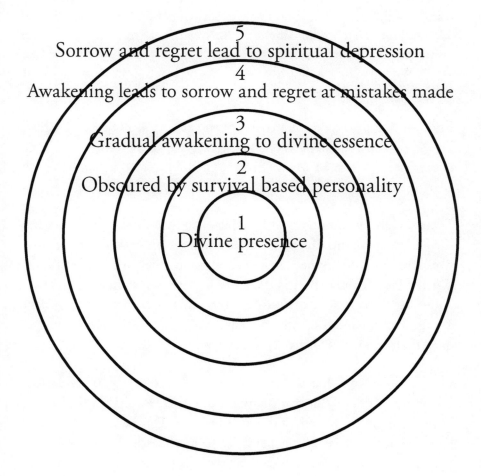

Sorrow and regret lead to spiritual depression

Awakening leads to sorrow and regret at mistakes made

Gradual awakening to divine essence

Obscured by survival based personality

Divine presence

Figure Nine

This concept may seem strange, even masochistic, to our "feel good" society. But other cultures have understood this process well. For example, in Renaissance Florence, many of the homes had a garden in the back called a Saturn garden. Saturn is the planet associated with the old and the dying. It represents creative disintegration, the leveling of the old before something new can emerge. When people were grieving either the death of a loved one or -- more to the point -- the death of a stage of life, they would sit in their Saturn garden and *no one would bother them*. That is the difference between societies that have some awareness of the spiritual growth process and a shallow society like ours. We have no tolerance for pain of any kind, even pain that is at the service of new life.

I do not like pain any more than anyone else. I am not a masochist. However, spiritual depression, at the service of new life, is a holy occurrence. We need to see it through to the freedom and the joy waiting on the other side.

Theoretically, we do not need to experience this inner pain. If we are surrendering voluntarily, then no barrier is set up to begin with. In a similar way, we do not need to be depressed in order to grow spiritually. But the fact of the matter is that very few of us surrender voluntarily and most of us feel, at one time or the other, a deep disappointment at ourselves for mistakes that we have made. This disappointment at oneself almost inevitably leads to depression.

One would think that a depression would finally get our attention. For some, it does. But, for many people, this is only the first act in bringing about the rebirth of the authentic self. For these people, myself included, it is as if we must experience the total death of the inauthentic self before something greater can emerge. This next section of the book will describe what this "tearing down" of the inauthentic self both looks like and feels like. It is not a pretty picture. However, let us always keep the big picture in mind. It is all worth it. All of the pain, all of the demolition of the old self, leads inevitably to the discovery of our inner riches. With that perspective, let us examine what inauthentic living can do to our bodies.

III. THE DEATH OF THE INAUTHENTIC SELF

CHAPTER SEVEN

The Body Never Lies

Returning to our center does not imply a flight from the body. However, folks beginning the spiritual journey sometimes make it sound that way. You will hear things said like, "I could be more spiritual if only I could quit worrying about my body". If we have ever thought that way, it indicates that we have a misconception of the body's role as we grow spiritually.

The body is not an appendage, an obstacle to be overcome. The body is us. Every cell of our body is charged with divinity. When Christians say that the body is a temple of the Holy Spirit, this does not mean that the body houses a vapor-like puff of smoke called a spirit. The body is a dimension, the mind another, and the spirit still another. But the *person* is not fragmented that way. We *are* a body/mind/spirit. We are *one*.

Much of the misconception about the role of the body goes back to two philosophical points of view called Gnosticism and Manichaeism. The Gnostics and the Manichaens advocated repressing anything having to do with the body, especially sex.

The "official" Judeo-Christian teaching on this matter has always been clear. The body is good. Bodily functions, including sex and reproduction, are good. In fact, everything in creation is good.

I put the word "official" in quotes because Gnostic and Manichaen tendencies have often crept back into religious popular teachings about the body. One of the worst incursions in recent centuries was a point of view called Jansenism. Basically, this was a warmed-over version of the old Manichaean hatred of the body. Jansenistic strains became fairly widespread in Europe, especially in France and Ireland. Because so many of the clergy that came to America were French or Irish, they brought with them this unhealthy attitude toward the human body. Some clergy still have it.

We simply do not know what to do with the body on this spiritual journey of ours. We have often become so alienated from our bodies that we are not even sure what they have to do with spirituality. It is almost as if the body is an embarrassment, totally irrelevant, at best, to our spiritual growth.

There is an old saying that goes, "What you resist, will persist." Try to ignore the body and it will double its efforts to get our attention. What does it wish to tell us? It wishes to give us a report on the status of things on subtler levels of our being. It is an accurate barometer of what is happening deep within us.

This understanding of the human person comes from something called the Perennial Philosophy. This is very important to our discussion here. The Perennial Philosophy deals with what has always been understood by the most mature mystics from the beginning of time. This is truth that transcends individual religious expression. One of the things that has been universally believed by the mystics of the world is that the universe is composed of a Great Chain of Being. The universe is structured, or has aspects, which are traditionally called physical, mental-emotional, and spiritual. But is all connected to God or, more precisely, is God in various forms of matter, mind and spirit. The chain looks like this.

The Great Chain of Being

1. Pure Spirit

2. Higher Mental-concepts, universal laws

3. Lower Mental-thoughts

4. Higher Emotional-love, joy

5. Lower Emotional- fear, anger

6. Etheric-energy body

7. Physical-physical body

I am committed in this book to keeping things simple, concrete, and understandable, so I do not want to go off on a metaphysical tangent. But I do think it is important to list the Great Chain of Being so that we have some philosophical basis for talking about the interconnection between the body and the rest of who we are.

What the Great Chain of Being implies is that the physical manifestation is the final one. By the time that things have "descended" to that level, much has been going on for a long time. For example, one does not just "get" a headache out of the clear blue sky. Tension and stress have been stirring for some time. Or perhaps one is experiencing mental fatigue from too much thinking about the past.

The body is, as it were, the "last to know." By the time something has become somatized – i.e., expressed at the physical level as a bodily symptom - this represents a culmination of things that have been percolating for some time. All of this is to say that our physical health or lack thereof can often tell us something about the state of our souls. (see Figure 10)

The Body Never Lies

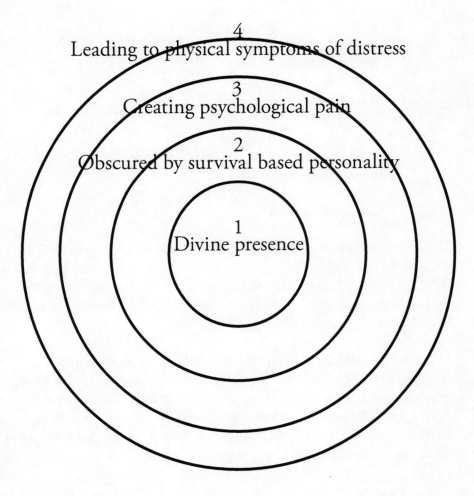

4
Leading to physical symptoms of distress

3
Creating psychological pain

2
Obscured by survival based personality

1
Divine presence

Figure Ten

We have to be careful here. I am going to say something and then repeat it again later in this chapter: illness is a mystery. There are so many variables here that can alter the equation. What is the health history of the individuals' family? What toxins might the individual have been exposed to in the environment? What about the availability or lack of availability of preventive health care? What about proper nutrition? What about genetic predisposition? And so on. What I am trying to say here is that we need to be very, very cautious about assuming why someone has gotten sick.

There is a tendency today by some to play a little game called "blame the victim." Whenever someone gets ill, you are liable to find all sorts of self-styled "experts" who think they have it all figured out as to how and why the individual has gotten ill. Let us spell it out loud and clear here: we can never be sure why any of us may have contracted an illness. There are simply too many variables to ever be sure.

That having been said, the Great Chain of Being, along with the insights of holistic medicine, along with common sense, tell us that there is often a manifestation on the bodily level of some imbalance found on a subtler level of our being. This is what is known as a psychosomatic illness. Let us now examine what a psychosomatic illness is all about.

Listening to the Body

One of the great things about the body is that it never lies. It is always trying to tell us something about ourselves.

Of course, sometimes the only message that the body has to communicate is that it has just caught the flu or some other communicable disease. With such illnesses, a person's mental condition has little to do with what the body is experiencing.

Often, however, there is a very close connection between one's illness and the inner struggles one is going through. This is what is called a psychosomatic illness.

Sometimes persons mistakenly think that a psychosomatic illness is just a figment of one's mind. Nothing could be farther from the truth. A psychosomatic illness is very real, but it is caused not by a virus, or wound, or infection, but by some inner turmoil that is bothering the person.

How common are these psychosomatic illnesses? I have seen estimates that claim as much as eighty percent of our illnesses are of this nature. I heard one doctor say that he would have to close up shop if his work were confined solely to problems unrelated to the psyche.

The top five killers in this country are heart attacks, cancer, substance abuse, suicide, and accidents. Stress has been linked to heart attacks and indirectly linked to cancer. And it is pretty clear that substance abuse and suicide are associated with persons in trouble. Strangely enough, there is even a link between stress and accidents. Persons who are preoccupied are much more likely to be involved in serious accidents.

The message is clear: We should listen to our bodies. What are our bodies trying to tell us about what is going on inside us?

There is nothing morally wrong about having a psychosomatic illness. Its presence simply indicates that we do not have it "all together." It just means we are human.

I once did some research on the religious conversion of St. Augustine. Apparently he was a victim of a psychosomatic illness that affected his chest area. Augustine used to make his living with his lungs. He was a great teacher of rhetoric, but gradually came to see his career as a hollow vocation.

As the moment of his spiritual conversion grew closer, the pain in his chest got more excruciating. It was almost as if his body were telling him that a life of rhetoric was not for him. Immediately after his conversion, his chest pain disappeared.

My own experience with psychosomatic illnesses has proved to be a major part of my spiritual journey. Always my pattern has been the same. Psychosomatic illnesses have gotten my attention, they have mirrored what the real underlying issues were, and they have gone away when my crisis was eventually resolved.

My first psychosomatic ailment occurred two weeks after my thirtieth birthday. Of course, I never made the connection between my ailment – back pain – and turning thirty. In my mind, there was no connection at all. It was just a coincidence.

There had been no history of back pain in my family. I had never experienced any difficulties there beforehand. But now there was this nagging, energy-draining condition that was sapping the quality from my life. I mentioned earlier that there are two types of people in this world: those who have back pain and those who don't. For those who have experienced such pain, nothing further need be said. For those who have never had such pain, no explanation will suffice. The pain is constant and unrelenting. You do not even really sleep at night. You just sort of pass out.

Of course, I did everything that I could think of to take away the pain. I went to osteopaths, orthopods, chiropractors, massage therapists, and yoga instructors. Absolutely nothing gave me anything but temporary, symptomatic relief. At one point, I seriously contemplated a back operation. One of my doctors, the orthopod, said that I had a slight scoliosis, a curvature of the spine. The x-rays had revealed it. I suppose if you study x-rays of the back long enough, you will eventually find something. After all, no one is cosmetically perfect. In any event, I latched onto this explanation. Something objective, something out of my control, something that was not my fault. This sounded more palatable to me. Maybe that was what was causing the pain. In desperation, I almost went along with his recommendation. In hindsight, I can now see this for the disaster it would have been. But, at the time, I was willing to go along with almost any recommendation which held out hope for relief.

For some reason that I may never fully understand, I rejected the suggestion for surgery. The pain, however, did not go away. On the contrary, it got worse. All of this came to a head during the summer of 1976. Before that summer, believe it or not, I had not even been depressed before, let alone having ever experienced a serious physical ailment. I was now thirty-one and a half years of age.

In a state of helplessness, primarily due to my back pain, I remember falling to my knees and saying something like, "Ok, God, I surrender. You win. Whoever you are, if you exist, I give up." What was curious about this statement was that this was the first time in a year and a half that I had even remotely considered the possibility that the back pain had anything to do with deeper issues. Up until then, it was as if this back pain had invaded me from outer space. And it was the job of some specialist to take it away.

When I got up from my knees, I was shocked to feel that the back pain had gone away totally. I have never felt more joy or more gratitude about anything in my life before or since.

Immediately my rational mind went to work to try to figure out what had happened. The best that I could come up with at that time was that Jesus had healed me. Jesus as an entity, a person, although a person in spirit. I reasoned that he had done this because I had turned my life over to him and his father. The people in the retreat house where I was staying shared this explanation, more or less, so I bought into it, even though something never felt right about my understanding of what happened.

I now have a very different explanation for what happened. First of all, I don't think there was anything coincidental about my back pain. It came about as a result of a young man trying to carry on his back the responsibilities of the world. Trying to be perfect, trying to sublimate my legitimate sexual needs, trying to please everyone, carrying around repressed anger for my plight and feeling guilty because I was angry about it all, the weight of the world was "breaking my back." As I write

94

this, I am looking at a statue of Atlas, one of my favorite characters from mythology. The world looks heavy to him as it bends his back. The world felt heavy to me, too.

What I think happened is that I finally took the weight of the world off of my shoulders. In saying that I "gave it to Jesus," this is a way of saying that I gave my life over to a higher power. I thereafter felt a part of a whole. The whole was now in charge. I was just an atom in the body of the world. It was no longer just up to me. I was no longer the center, the ultimate arbiter and decider of what should happen.

At first glance, this can seem like an alienating, splitting experience. However, the effect was just the opposite. Finding my center entailed finding my true self, to be sure, but it also involved situating that center in a reality much larger than myself. All of this did not constitute a miracle. Instead, it was a kind of healing, a returning to the center, a realignment of my place in the universe. The change in consciousness has been permanent, even deepening, with at least one major exception.

The exception arose when I chose to say no to the ongoing evolution of my life. That first surrender was all about an inner change in consciousness. My next challenge, much more threatening to me, involved a change in the way I was living my life. Specifically, it was about a calling from within to leave my career as a Christian minister.

The threatening feelings came from the fact that I was in my 40's when I began to feel, once again, a kind of divine discontent. My response was typical of the response of many people: denial. In an attempt to avoid dealing with this call, I threw myself into my work even more than before. The reason that I was so threatened by what I sensed stirring within me was that I knew that any decision to move on would entail giving up a way of life that I knew very well, a life that promised me lifetime security.

Never underestimate the power of the promise of security. People will sacrifice their self-respect, sometimes even their souls, for security.

Healer Carolyn Myss speaks of the archetype of the Inner Prostitute, the part of us that will let go of our dreams in life in order to have someone or something take care of us. The Church had been taking care of me since I began studying for the ministry as a teenager. Most of my major life decisions were made for me. As long as I went along with the program, I could always count on more of the same.

My particular situation was complicated by the fact that I was also very well known, popular, and unusually affluent for a person in church ministry. My affluence came from the fact that I was a speaker in demand all over the country. I had been a regular lecturer on television, had written two books, and had my own newspaper column. Why is this important to my story? Because, deep within me, I knew that, if I resigned from the ministry, all of this would end instantaneously. I would be cut off, shunned, and blackballed. All invitations to speak at churches, on television, and retreat houses would either end immediately or be cancelled as soon as the hierarchy found out what I was doing.

All of this might be hard to believe in the new millennium, but that is precisely what often still happens. I knew that I would be cut off from a pension, given no severance pay, and would become part of the "enemy" overnight. A major part of me wanted nothing to do with leaving the ministry, because I would be out on the street, without marketable skills, with no financial support, and with the overt threat that I would never be welcome in any church institution.

It was not hard for me to resist this call, given the consequences. But there was a commercial that happened to be on television that put it this way, "It's not nice to fool Mother Nature". If you are not living a life of integrity, if you are living off-center, the same thing eventually happens to all of us: we get sick. The sickness may be depression, which often stems from the fact that we are angry at ourselves because we are being unfaithful to who we are called to be. Or we may suffer burnout. Or - and this is the point of the chapter - we may very well get physically sick. This had been my pattern before. Why should it be any different this time?

The first physical ailment that life then sent me to get my attention was arthritis in my fingers and toes. I celebrated the sacraments and wrote with my hands and traveled around the country (and the world) on my feet, so why should I not feel pain there? On top of that, arthritis is often associated with repressed anger. I was angry, frustrated at my plight, so arthritis became my symptom.

Friends and family members were too close to the situation to see the obvious. So their feedback to me centered around the fact that, since I was at that time in my forties, what did I expect? People that age get arthritis. Don't read into things. What is the big deal? You are just getting older.

Such feedback was music to my ears. Just like the back pain had come from "out there", so had the arthritis. It was an ailment that I had "caught". I just needed the right specialist with the right magic elixir. Then it would all go away. Of course, it did not go away at all. It just went underground and surfaced again in an additional manner. This time my soul created another symptom in addition to the arthritis: TMJ (tempo mandibular joint syndrome). In other words, I was grinding my teeth at night.

Carl Jung says that life will begin by giving us hints. If we do not take the first hint, the hints will start getting stronger. Did I see any of this at the time? Of course not. Like many people, I am a very poor physician when trying to heal myself. But, since the pain was at the service of life, and not a punishment, my soul gave me another gift: a ruptured Achilles' tendon.

The response to both of these angels of healing was the same: denial and rationalization. My "solution" to the TMJ was to buy a rubber mold to put on my teeth at night. No one in my family had ever had a history of TMJ. For that matter, no one had ever had arthritis either. But none of these facts deterred me. "The enemy was outside myself. These things happen. You ruptured your Achilles' heel because you did not stretch properly before playing basketball. And what are you doing playing basketball at forty-five?"

The symbolism of the ruptured Achilles' heel was hard for even me to miss. I can remember attending a lecture at one of our local Jungian study groups when I had just had my accident. I walked into the room in a cast, on crutches, with a ruptured Achilles' heel. Of course, my Jungian friends jumped on that one like a batter jumping on a hanging curve ball. "What is your Achilles' heel, Tom? What is life trying to tell you?"

I imagine most people are aware of the story of Achilles from Greek mythology. In a nutshell, his mother had dipped him into a river that would ensure his invincibility. But she held him by his Achilles' tendon when she did so. Thus, the only part of him that had not been exposed to the river of invincibility were those tendons. Later, in battle, Achilles was indeed invincible. Arrows would bounce off of him without doing him any damage. Then one day an arrow happened to hit him on that tendon connecting his leg to his foot. When it did, he collapsed like a sack of potatoes. The Achilles heel has since come to symbolize one's point of vulnerability. The symbolism in my case was exquisite. I, the mighty one, had my points of vulnerability after all.

In case you are interested, my points of vulnerability were twofold: 1) my understanding of truth had overflowed a Christian container, and I needed a larger container; and 2) I was ready for a partner in life. Denying these two requirements of my soul was breaking me down system by system. I have no way of being able to prove this, but I believe that my next wake-up call from life would have been either a heart attack or an automobile accident.

Finally, at last, I recognized that I was in inner distress. So I began intensive psychological therapy. Never underestimate the power of denial, even while in the midst of therapy. I had certainly perfected denial to an art form. Let me give an example that illustrates that point very clearly. After one of my sessions, when it was becoming clear to me that my soul was inviting me to move beyond the institutional church, I was still in deep denial. Leaving one of my sessions, my therapist escorted me to the door. I was still in a cast and on crutches because of my ruptured Achilles tendon. At the doorstep, I remember saying, "I don't want to leave the ministry. I feel like I am in full stride in my life right now." With a warm smile, my therapist looked at my cast and crutches and said, "You don't look like you're in full stride to me, Tom." Never in my life, before or since, have I felt more naked, more exposed, more "found out." I could feel my face flushing with embarrassment.

I did not want to face reality at that time in my life. My inner needs and my lofty ideals and my ego and my hormones were all in conflict. I was at war within myself. Thank God I finally got the message. I have no way of proving this, of course, but I am convinced that – if I had not finally gotten the message with the ruptured Achilles tendon – my next hints from life probably would have been more intense. I think that perhaps a heart attack or an automobile accident (which I almost had) would have eventually gotten my attention.

I realize that there is resistance within us in facing the whole phenomenon of psychosomatic illness. Part of this comes from our defense mechanism of denial. Part of it comes from our sensitivity to this phenomenon of blaming those who are sick. Part of our resistance, however, comes from the fact that we still live within a paradigm that tends to think that the mind and the body have very little to do with one another. Where did this kind of thinking originate? And how is the paradigm shifting today?

Mind as Healer

Ever since the days of the Enlightenment (the historical period following the Renaissance) there has been widespread mistrust between medicine and those holding a spiritual perspective. Doctors have often judged spiritual claims to be unscientific, and spiritual leaders have often been distrustful of science because it seemed that the unknown was being left out of the picture.

But today there is dialogue between the medical and the spiritual model, in part because of important research in the area of psychosomatic illnesses. Doctors have always been aware that a good attitude toward life can color our emotions and brighten up a part of our day. But what about the stark reality of disease? Is our mental attitude partially responsible for the development of serious disease? And, even more interesting, can the powers of the mind contribute to the healing of diseases?

Kenneth R. Pelletier, Ph.D., assistant clinical professor at Langley Porter Neuropsychiatric Institute in San Francisco, is convinced that the human spirit does indeed profoundly influence our physical health. Dr. Pelletier wanted to know why a small percentage of individuals with "incurable" diseases somehow are healed of their illnesses. His personal interviews with a sampling of those who had been "miraculously cured" revealed the following findings.

All those who had recovered despite great odds had experienced:

- Profound intrapsychic changes. That is, their innermost being had been reshaped in some way by meditation, prayer, or some other spiritual practice.

- Profound interpersonal changes. Their relations with other persons had been placed on a new and more solid footing.

- Significant alterations in diet. These persons no longer took their food for granted. They were conscious of nutrition and carefully watched what they ate.

- A deep sense of the spiritual, as opposed to the purely material, facets of life.

Dr. Pelletier is now convinced that a spiritual orientation in life actually improves one's physical health. He is by no means alone; countless other physicians have come to the same conclusion.

Psychologists, too, are coming to terms with the psychic benefits of spirituality. In fact, there is a whole new school in psychology (spiritual psychology) that is convinced a person cannot be a full human without some openness to the spiritual dimension.

With medicine and psychology now comparing notes with those on the spiritual journey, where do we go from here? It appears that the human endeavor may be on the brink of a great breakthrough. Instead of physicians and psychologists and spiritual teachers competing with one another, we may be in for a period of unprecedented cooperation. Those with spiritual proficiency will be seen as equal partners in the healing professions.

Dr. David Breslan of the U.C.L.A. pain control unit notes that the ancient Chinese distinguished five levels of physicians: Lowest was the veterinarian or animal doctor. Next came the doctor who used acupuncture to relieve specific complaints (symptomatic medicine). Third was the surgeon, who treated more serious health problems. Second highest was the nutritionist, who practiced preventive medicine by teaching what to eat. But highest of all was the philosopher-sage, who taught people the order of the universe. He was the only doctor who could directly effect a genuine cure, by going right to the heart of the problem: the patient's ignorance of how to live harmoniously with nature.

I realize that we are always in danger of oversimplifying here. For example, a five-year-old girl who comes down with cancer after being exposed to carcinogens in the drinking water is an innocent victim. Illness is, when all is said and done, a mystery. There are so may variables that we can never be absolutely sure why anyone gets sick or stays well. After having stated that caveat, however, it is also true that the body is intimately associated with the mind and with the human spirit. They all work together as a holy Trinity of wholistic health. Physical illness, as well as wellbeing often tells us much about the health of our inner being.

Illness as an Opportunity

One final point needs to be made about illness and the spiritual path. An incurable illness can be an opportunity for growth. I will go into this in more depth in Chapter Nine, in the section on "Sickness and Dying." Here let us simply make the point that many people have grown spiritually as a result of an incurable illness.

Teilhard de Chardin often spoke of the "diminishments" in life. What he was referring to was the fact that certain events in life serve to strip away the non-essentials. In the process, our essence is revealed to us. An incurable illness or injury can be like that. When the actor Christopher Reeve, who played Superman, was paralyzed as a result of his injury, he originally went through a period of denial when he convinced himself that other people had been known to rebound from similar accidents, and that he would be back to normal in a short period of time. When the reality of the gravity of this condition set in, he said that he began to disidentify from his body as the essence of who he was. When you have been literally wearing the cape of Superman for much of your grown life, that is not the easiest thing in the world to do. However, he eventually realized that he was still Christopher Reeve, even though he could not even stand up on his own, let alone leap tall buildings at a single bound. He had managed to identify with his soul, of which the body was only the vehicle. The diminishment of his bodily abilities had paradoxically revealed to him more of his core self.

Let us look at another analogy to make the point. One of the most memorable parts of the novel <u>The Agony and the Ecstasy</u> comes when Michelangelo is portrayed as describing how he carves a statue out of marble. He said that he begins by allowing the marble to "speak" to him and to tell him what figure is already in the stone straining to reveal itself. When Michelangelo feels that he knows what figure is within the stone, he begins to chip away all of the marble that does not belong there anymore. As the piece of marble is diminished of its non-essentials, the core figure within the stone becomes apparent.

Life often seems to do a similar thing with us, and perhaps in no way more that when our physical abilities are taken away from us. As the body loses its power and abilities and vitality, people often get in touch with their core self that has been frozen in stone for most of a lifetime. When it happens that way, an incapacity, physical illness, or condition can be a catalyst for a spiritual awakening.

What more do we need to get our attention that something is amiss in our lives? If depression does not do it, and having the various systems of our body break down, what will it take? For some people, again including myself, it may take an onslaught of self-destructive, suicidal thoughts before we come to the realization that we are in need of a Higher Power. Our next chapter deals with suicidal ideation, something that is a lot more common than many people realize. Let us now examine this phenomenon in light of what it may mean in the journey back to divine consciousness.

CHAPTER EIGHT

suicide

Writing about suicide in the context of the spiritual journey is a very delicate matter. For one thing, I do not wish to imply that every suicidal ideation or attempt is at the service of the true self. Clearly it is not. However, on the other hand, I have seen and experienced enough examples where suicide has spiritual elements to it that the issue needs to be treated in this book.

The best way to handle the topic, in my estimation, is to, first of all, briefly examine some of the instances where suicidal tendencies are *not* contributory towards spiritual growth. The last thing that I would want to do here would be to oversimplify this complex subject. Nor would I want to "glorify" suicidal thoughts. Suicidal thoughts can be nightmarish and often need to be treated psychiatrically. But yet…but yet…there are those other times when suicidal thoughts are at the service of new life. Let us try to get a handle on this important aspect of spiritual growth. When is suicidal ideation a totally negative situation and when is it part of the unfolding of something more beautiful from within us?

Sorting Things Out

Today is April 28, 1999. As I sit down to write the first draft of this chapter on suicide, I am staring at a headline from today's Philadelphia Inquirer which says, "Oklahoma City bombing is still claiming lives." It is a story about six people close to the bombing who have committed suicide since the 1995 tragedy. Suicide happens. It is a fact of life. Most people reading this probably know of someone who has committed suicide. The questions to be answered are: 1) why does it happen?; and 2) more to the point, what does a chapter on suicide have to do with growing spiritually?

Suicide happens for many reasons. One obvious reason would be a physical one. For example, Charles Whitman, the young man who, years ago, shot all of those people from the bell tower at the University of Texas was found, when autopsied, to have a brain tumor. Never underestimate the role of the physical dimension to explain much of human behavior. People can do something as irrational as killing themselves or others due to brain and nervous system abnormalities.

A situation close to brain and nervous system irregularities would be unbearable pain. Everyone has their breaking point. There is only so much that people can take. If someone feels that ending their life will bring about a cessation of pain, one could certainly understand why they might choose to go ahead with that course of action. Torture of prisoners, for example, almost always brings about its desired effect. If the pain is great enough, people will do almost anything to stop it. They will give away state secrets, they will betray loved ones, and they will put the barrel of a gun in their mouths and pull the trigger. The desire to live at all costs is often outweighed by the price of enduring excruciating pain.

Another cause of suicide is deep, situational depression. The example of the Oklahoma City bombing survivors is a case in point. In this instance, we are most likely dealing with an example of "survivor's guilt." Those who survived are initially grateful for being alive. As one of those survivors put it, "God really must have been watching over me." The gratitude eventually turns to guilt as the person begins to wonder why he was spared while others died. This anger turned against the self is one of the classical causes of depression. If the anger is strong enough, it can turn to self-hatred, which then turns to despair, which then turns to thoughts of self-destruction. Sometimes the thoughts are acted upon, resulting in the ultimate "acting out" of suicide.

There are many other forms of situational depression besides the above-cited examples of "survivor's guilt." One situation that could drive a person to suicide would be the feeling that one is in an absolutely untenable position, a cul-de-sac from which there is no apparent escape. For example, a married man falls head over heels in love with another woman. Every fiber of his being wants to be with his lover. But, perhaps, his religious and moral values prohibit him from leaving his wife and children. He feels checkmated. He feels there is no way out except to end his own life.

Let's look at another example of situational guilt. A pillar of the community and a deacon of his church is shown to be a pedophile. Or a crossdresser. Or an embezzler. Whatever the charge, if it is felt to be so shameful that the man cannot bear to face his family, friends, and community, the man might take his own life. When such upstanding citizens are publicly charged, they may not have the inner resources to be able to live with the consequent change in their public image and status. They then look for a quick way out of their misery. Suicide seems like their only alternative.

People will sometimes commit suicide over a great loss. Let's say that a man and a woman have been together for forty years. They cannot imagine life without the other. When one dies, the other decides to follow. Whatever might be our assessment as to how healthy this response might be, the fact is that this sort of thing happens. Perhaps it happens more often than people realize.

Besides all of these actual suicides that can and do take place, there are also suicide attempts that are actually more "cries for help." In these cases, the individual is not actually intent on killing him or herself, but is, rather, doing something dramatic that is designed to get the attention of loved ones. The plan of the suicide has been unconsciously set up to fail. The individual is reasonably certain that someone will be there to rescue him before the deed is carried to its completion.

While it may seem as if it is only a cry for help, the presumption must always be made that the attempt is a serious one. There is too much at stake to do otherwise. It is literally a matter of life and death. That is why therapists are taught that suicidal plans by their clients are justification for intervention by the therapist. Even the sacred practice of confidentiality between therapist and client may be violated in such cases. Extreme circumstances justify extreme responses. One must take the threats seriously and respond accordingly.

Hopefully, by now, two things are clear to the reader: 1) the reasons for a person committing suicide are varied and complex; and 2) all threats concerning suicide should be taken seriously. That having been said, I would now like to explore a type of suicidal ideation that is very little understood: egocide. This is where the spiritual aspect of suicide enters the picture.

Egocide

From a spiritual point of view, there is a kind of death that actually leads to new life. I am referring to the "death" of the survival personality. As we have seen earlier, popular parlance sometimes uses the word "ego" when it wishes to refer to what we have called, in this book, the "survival personality". Ego, according to our definition, should never die. It represents the part of us that has an individual identity, the part that we refer to when we say "I". Of course, for most of us, our sense of "I" has been fractured and degraded to the point where we think that this fear-based survival personality of ours is the true self. So, for our purposes of discussion, let us use the word ego the way it is commonly used, as the part of us that thinks in terms of fear, lack, and separation.

In order for us to grow spiritually, this part of us must "die". Please forgive another qualifier, but it is easy to misunderstand what is required of us here. The point is not to kill the survival personality (or ego); the point is to transform it. That having been said, it is okay to use the word "die" because, when we are going through the process of transformation, it may actually *feel* like we are dying. So it is legitimate, in this context, to say that our ego must die if we are to grow spiritually. (see Figure 11)

Notice the use of the word "must" here. Death of the false self, death of the ego, is not optional. It is not a rule we are dealing with, but a law. It is written into the very nature of things.

As I write these words, there are hundreds of birds singing outside my balcony. The grass is turning green again. That is because *"E l' Aprile"* (it is April). The words of that Italian aria go through my head as I contemplate the glory of spring. But the spring arises from the dead of winter. The earth had to die first before it could be reborn. Funny, it happens that way every year. Maybe nature is trying to tell us something. Maybe it is trying to tell us that death is okay, even necessary, when it is at the service of new life. Of course that is the truth.

This is what Jesus means when he says that "unless the grain of wheat die and fall into the earth, it will bear no fruit." What he is saying, psychologically, is that unless the survival personality (the ego) loses its grip and is reintegrated in the unconscious, a person will never discover the true self that lies within.

Hinduism also sings the glory of death. Obviously, it is not singing the glory of physical death. Such a death, by itself, accomplishes nothing. It is singing the glory that can come after the death of the survival personality (the ego). The goddess Kali, with her many hands, each one carrying symbols of destruction, does the divine work of dismantling the old self. She destroys all of the illusions of the false self, slicing and killing all within us that needs to die.

109

Suicide

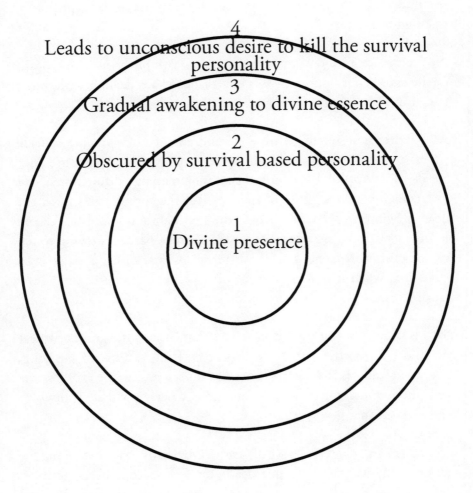

4
Leads to unconscious desire to kill the survival
personality

3
Gradual awakening to divine essence

2
Obscured by survival based personality

1
Divine presence

Figure Eleven

It is my firm belief that this form of egocide is a holy process. Unfortunately, very few people understand how sacred the work is. With their shortsighted approach to the process of spiritual growth, they tend to view all pain as bad. It is not. Pain and death are perfectly fine, not as an end unto themselves, but as the price of new life in all its forms.

Let us take another example, that of childbirth. Pain is a part of the process of giving birth to new life. Granted, the inevitable pain can turn into suffering as our fears get in the way. That is the purpose of classes for prospective parents. They are taught how to relax as much as possible, how to breathe, how to go with the flow. All of this can do much to minimize the pain associated with childbirth. However, even when this is done as well as possible, I think it is fair to say that giving birth is no picnic. Be that as it may, what mother begrudges the pain when she holds to her breast the fruit of all that pain? A husband told me a story that makes a point here. His wife had a very, very difficult delivery. She was in tears, in agony. But, as soon as she held the baby to her the first time, she said to her husband, only half kidding, "Let's have another one!"

The wise therapist or soul friend knows that inevitably there will be some pain involved in giving birth to the true self within us, just as there is in giving birth to a baby. In fact, one of my favorite metaphors for a good soul guide is that of a midwife. Think of the image. The midwife does not create the baby or even the process of giving birth. That happens according to some higher plan. And the midwife is not capable of taking away all pain, either. She can reduce needless suffering due to fear, but the mother is the real hero. She will have to withstand a certain amount of pain. No one can do that for her. The midwife's job is actually a simple one: it is to facilitate the birth of something not of its making, minimizing needless suffering, and coaching the individual to see the inevitable pain in the context of the new life emerging. A spiritual coach should do all of the above, just in a different realm, the realm of the death of the old self and the birth of the new self.

How sad it is when this is not understood. How sad it is when we try to short-circuit the whole process by taking away people's pain prematurely. An example comes to mind. Let us call this person Joan. Here was an individual on the brink, in my opinion, of a major spiritual breakthrough. Of course, the breaking down and the deconstruction of the old self had to happen first. Kali had to "do her thing" before Joan could experience the miracle of experiencing her inner beauty. But no one around her had the foggiest notion of anything about this process. They only had this limited, well-intentioned but myopic, goal of eliminating all pain for everyone under all circumstances.

I will never forget the sight of Joan walking to greet me in the psych-ward of the hospital. That is where her family had her placed. Joan came walking towards me in a kind of shuffle that mental health professionals have nicknamed the "Thorazine shuffle." The feet hardly lift off of the floor. The eyes are glazed over to the point where it looks as if "no one is home." There was Joan, in her slippers and her pajamas and her bathrobe walking toward me. The medical establishment had done what it knows how to do: it stopped the pain as much as possible. Well intentioned, they had no way of knowing that they had intervened prematurely. They had short-circuited the process. They had postponed the inevitable.

Years later, the chickens finally came home to roost. The anti-psychotic medicine had succeeded in making Joan a kind of zombie, a member of the walking dead. She was able to function, but the spark was gone. The élan, the *joie de vivre*, the creativity, all gone. So when she finally broke down again ten years later (and somehow discovered her true self within), I could only conclude that all of this could have happened ten years earlier if there had been some soul doctors around, some people who had some inkling of how one grows spiritually.

Joan was initially hospitalized because she was beginning to talk about suicide. Perhaps that was the prudent thing to do at the time. But perhaps it was not. I have run into at least some situations in which treating the patient with anti-psychotic medication would be the last thing that was needed. I know this for sure because, at one point in my life, I was one such case.

My suicidal ideation came upon me suddenly during the summer of 1976. That was not a typical year for me. During that summer I went through the culmination of a death/rebirth experience that had been occurring for a year and a half, actually from the day that I turned 30 years of age. Distress happening around any age milestone should be a fairly strong clue that we are dealing with a spiritual issue here. After all, issues concerning meaning in life are inevitably spiritual in nature. But, typically, I missed the real significance around all of the stress that I was feeling. What did turning thirty have to do with anything? That is the way I was thinking at the time.

Specifically, a lot of things came together for me to deal with during the summer of 1976. I was dealing with: 1) turning thirty; 2) being a Christian minister and feeling a million miles away from God; 3) struggling with my vow of celibacy; 4) a psychosomatic illness of excruciating lower back pain; 5) a deep depression; and 6) a spiritual awakening. All of it was happening at once and it was overwhelming to me. Actually, I can see it now as really only one issue, spiritual emergence, with all of the other things happening being just pieces in a giant jigsaw puzzle. But, at the time, all I knew was that I was hurting and my life was overwhelming and I was feeling completely desperate and out of control.

When I look at the summation of what was going on, I can now say, "Of course it was a spiritual crisis!" But at the time I had no perspective and could not see anything. This blindness added to the problem. If you know what is happening to you, it seems to me that you can put up with just about anything. But if one is flying without vision, the whole ordeal can be terrifying.

My terror culminated one night while on a thirty-day retreat. There is that number thirty again. Never take a thirty-day retreat unless you are asking for trouble! Only kidding. But a retreat of that magnitude and duration will almost certainly allow for all of one's issues to coalesce and come to a head. While walking around the retreat house grounds, everything that I was dealing with came together within me and I could see only one way out: suicide. I can remember walking down to the water's edge, feeling its pull, ready to walk into the water and drown myself. For some reason, perhaps lack of courage or just the instinct of survival, I willed myself not to do it.

Years later, with the luxury of perspective, I now have some understanding as to what this was really all about. My soul was saying to my survival personality (ego): it is time for you to die. You have served me in your current state of consciousness for as long as you can. Thanks for the memories, but you have outlived your usefulness. The pain is too great. You can let go now. It is time for a new Tom Legere.

As a subsequent student of Jungian psychology, this perspective helped me to understand the situation even more. Water is always a symbol of the unconscious. Feeling drawn to drown myself in the ocean was the soul's metaphysical way of saying that it is necessary to let go of one's hold on everyday consciousness and explore one's depths, one's unconscious. The symbolism of it all was exquisite.

Later, my take on all of this was confirmed by a series of dreams that I had. For the next six months, I had the same recurring dream. I would walk up to the water's edge, barefoot, put my toes in, and then quickly pull back like a little child pulls back from an incoming wave. I took this to mean that I was currently beginning to get ready to do some deep inner work, but I was still afraid to "take the plunge".

I certainly do not wish to imply that every thought about suicide is actually a metaphor about the death of the ego (egocide). I think that my introductory remarks in this chapter make that fact abundantly clear. But I am convinced that at least *sometimes* that is the case. And the medical establishment does not know what to do about this when it happens. Due to a training almost totally devoid of spiritual content (this is just *beginning* to change), mostly everyone in the medical and psychological community immediately jumps to the conclusion that the pain must be stopped now. Rather than be midwives of new psychological life, they choose to terminate the new life by stopping the process before it has had a chance to come to completion.

There are tiny pockets of hope around this issue. One that comes to mind is the advent of programs for medical students which try to introduce them to the religious/spiritual side of their future patients. Future psychiatrists are among this new crop of medical students. This is a step in the right direction. However, from what I have seen, the programs deal almost exclusively with the religious side while ignoring the spiritual growth process. There is nothing ill intentioned in any of this. It is just that the people they are bringing in to do these programs do not have any understanding of spirituality as distinct from religion. Teaching about the practices of Christianity or Orthodox Judaism or any institutional religion is very interesting, but what does it have to do with the contents of this book? What light does it shine upon the survival personality, spiritual depression and egocide?

The very best work being done to educate people, both professional and otherwise, is being done in the field of transpersonal psychology (a.k.a. spiritual psychology). Actually there are some subtle differences between transpersonal and spiritual psychology, but they are both dedicated to exploring higher forms of consciousness, not as pathologies, but as the natural birthright of all human beings. From what I can see, these folks are not the ones being tapped to educate our future mental health professionals.

The pioneering academic work in understanding the spiritual implications of mental breakdown has been done by a husband and wife team: Stanislas and Christina Grof. In particular, they have written two books, which I enthusiastically recommend as a follow-up to this chapter. The first of their books, written in 1989, is called Spiritual Emergency. A sequel to their first book is called The Stormy Search for the Self, written in 1992. Both books go into detail about the similarities and the differences between a psychotic break, which leads nowhere, and a spiritual awakening, which often looks like a psychotic break, but which turns out to be a state of consciousness which is at the service of new life.

The Grofs have even pioneered what they call The Spiritual Emergence Network. This amounts to a list of mental health professionals from around the world who have some understanding of what spiritual emergence looks like with an individual. This network of professionals will do their best to discern whether or not a spiritual dimension is involved in a mental meltdown. If it is, they will treat the emergency accordingly. If it is not, they will recommend more traditional treatments. Information about the Spiritual Emergence Network can be found in both of their books.

Over the years, as I have lectured about suicide vs. egocide, it never ceases to amaze me as to how many people share with me that they have contemplated suicide at one time or the other in their lives. They often regret how they were treated and ask the question, "How come no one understood what was happening at the time?" I reassure them that everyone was doing what they thought best, but that the system did, in fact, fail them.

Suicide solves nothing. It does not even take away our pain. From what we have learned about near-death experiences, suicide just transfers the pain from one dimension to another. But egocide is another matter entirely. Such a process leads not to the dissolution of who we are, but only to the dissolution of who we *thought* we were. Waiting for us on the other side of the death is a rebirth, one that is more marvelous and freeing than anything that we ever thought possible.

We have seen, then, that suicidal thoughts *can be* a part of the spiritual journey. Hopefully this chapter helped to distinguish instances that need psychiatric intervention from those instances that are metaphors of the emergence of something new and beautiful from within us. Even though suicidal ideation is a lot more common than many people realize, it is still, I think, far from a universal experience. But what *does* seem to be universal, is some tearing down, in some way, of the survival personality. It is virtually impossible to mature spiritually without some *very* major bumps in the road.

Teilhard de Chardin spoke of the "diminishments" in life as a constructive force in spiritual evolution. In other words, some tearing down of the old forms is not only helpful but very much part of the process. Our next chapter will expand on this truth: that all that is valuable in life comes with a price tag associated with it. The ultimate thing of value, the pearl of great price, demands the ultimate sacrifice: letting go of who we have always thought that we were. Let us examine this process of break<u>down</u>, which, hopefully, can lead to a break<u>through</u>.

CHAPTER 9

The Breakdown Leading to a Breakthrough

One of the laws of the universe is that death is just as important as birth. In fact, nature itself tells us that all living things must die to their current forms. In a similar way, we humans never stay the same. Within seven years, every cell in our body changes. Why should we not change psychologically and spiritually as well?

When we look at nature, however, we see a tendency in all living things to cling to their current forms. Organisms usually do not die without a fight. A cornered rat, a wounded bear, a drowning victim fighting for breath, all tell us that – on the physical level – the instinct for survival is a strong one. It seems to me that the instinct for psychological survival is just as strong. We humans will cling to who we think we are because we do not know of any viable alternative.

On one level, there is a part of us deep within that still remembers that we are spirit. But this is so far buried within us that such a realization, for all practical purposes, is inaccessible to us. In order for us to access our divine consciousness once again, a consciousness that we had in an embryonic form as babies, the life force will have to overwhelm us.

Life will usually begin, as Carl Jung notes, by giving us hints. If we do not listen to the hints, the hints keep getting stronger. At a certain point in our lives, usually around mid-life, the life force is ready to make its move. It has seen that we are not picking up on the hints at all. It is time to get our attention in a strong way.

Before we can get to our essence, however, before we can return to the center, we need to break through whatever barnacles are covering our inner beauty. To a limited extent, we need to be proactive in this regard. This is where spiritual practice comes in. We can do things that work for us; things that help us get a glimpse of the beautiful part of us which is buried beneath the fear.

I am all in favor of regular spiritual practice. I do it myself and I find it to be crucial to my peace of mind and my development as a person. That having been said, however, I am a firm believer in the fact that often the journey undertakes *us*, rather than the other way around. In other words, just when it seems as if things are starting to go smoothly for us, the bottom falls out in our lives and we are on the journey whether we have chosen to be or not.

Most of us received very little preparation for the pain and the chaos involved in spiritual growth. One continues to grow throughout the life span, certainly, but as I remember what I was taught, I do not remember anyone telling me to expect experiences of trauma and breakdown and utter chaos. My only explanation for this gap in my education is that perhaps I was being prepared for religious indoctrination rather than spiritual growth. Because this much I know from experience: the journey to wholeness is very seldom a smooth one.

The two exceptions to this rule are the "once born" souls, as well as a group we could call "smooth evolvers." The "once born" souls are those who have always felt a deep closeness to God. There has never been strong ego resistance to begin with. These souls are still "in the garden," walking and talking with God, unaware of the shame that has driven the rest of us outside of the garden. Every once in a while I encounter such a soul. For some reason, they are usually little old ladies. They come up and speak to me after one of my lectures and say something like, "I don't have the slightest idea what you are talking about. I have always felt close to God. I am aware of the presence of the saints and the angels around me and I feel very much at peace." When they say this, I usually stand there with my mouth agape, not knowing what to say. I am speechless, because almost everyone that I know of seems to have a story to tell. Their journey has not been a smooth one. Many people I meet have been to hell and back.

Where do the exceptions to that rule originate? It seems to me that they have never developed a strong ego or a strong survival personality in the first half of life, so a strong counterpoint to Higher Power is never set up early in life. For, remember, tension and resistance is not set up by Higher Power. It is a function of the ego's desire to be independent, self-sufficient, and in control. Those "once born" souls apparently have no such desires. They have not had to do much surrendering because they have not rebelled to begin with.

While such persons do, indeed, exist, is it fair to speculate that they are very much in the minority? I think so. The great majority of us have not been so docile and compliant. No, we have grown into egohood (a good thing), but then our ego morphed into that creation we have called a survival personality. This hybrid creation quickly got set into a concrete mold. It served us well to some limited extent, but, at the beginning of the conscious spiritual path, it is now causing us pain. In fact, we could say that the pain caused by the survival personality *is* the start of the spiritual path.

The stage is set for something to happen, but what? It is no less than what feels like the demolition of the survival personality. It is the death of who we thought we were. An important distinction needs to be made here. Technically we do not die; we are transformed, like the butterfly. That having been said, however, the distinction often feels like a merely semantical one. For, when we are going through this demolition, this dismantling of who we thought we were, it often *feels like* we are dying. The semantical and theoretical distinctions do not offer us much comfort at a time like this. All we know is that our whole world is coming unraveled and we do not have the slightest idea at the time as to how it is all going to turn out. (see Figure 1)

The Dismantling Process

We are not in charge of the dismantling process; it is in charge of *us*. Just as the body goes through changes whether we welcome the changes or not, the psyche seems to work the same way. When it is time for the next stage to begin, the psyche – on its own – works out a way to take away our illusion of control. It does this through events that do not seem particularly spiritual at all. In fact, the events do not even seem helpful or positive at the time. These are events and outcomes to events that no person that I know would ever consciously choose. These occurrences, these experiences, cause us to question ourselves, with all of our preconceptions and assumptions about life. They serve to blast through our defenses or, at the very least, abrasively polish away our rough spots.

The Experience of Failure

For many of the topics in this chapter, I am indebted to Gerald O'Collins, S.J., who wrote a gem of a book entitled, *The Second Journey: Spirituality and the Mid Life Crisis.*[7] In the book, he lists some of the occurrences in life that serve to blast away our facades. One of these experiences is failure.

Failure may be an experience heretofore unknown to certain people in life. Oh sure, everyone makes little mistakes. That is why they put erasers on pencils. Nobody bats one thousand. However, here we are talking about something major not working out in life. If you have had a winning script since childhood, you will be unprepared for the process of "ego reduction" that happens when you are unable to accomplish something that you have set your heart on accomplishing. Let us take a look at some of the major areas where people experience major failure in life.

The Breakdown Leading to a Breakthrough

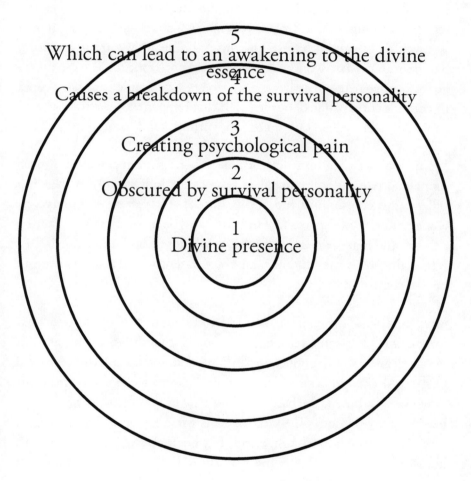

5
Which can lead to an awakening to the divine essence

4
Causes a breakdown of the survival personality

3
Creating psychological pain

2
Obscured by survival personality

1
Divine presence

Figure Twelve

Moral Failure

There are few things more unsettling, perhaps even psychologically devastating, than a major moral failure. At some time in our adult life, we usually feel that we have our moral compass generally pointed in the right direction. We have had our youthful indiscretions and have our scars to prove it. But we begin to feel that our moral code is fairly well established, maybe even interiorized. No mere external set of rules and regulations taught to us by our parents and other authority figures, it is now a set of values that we hold near and dear. We are in a groove, having found what works and what does not work for us. So far so good, but what happens if we now violate a principle that has been a linchpin, a cornerstone of our lives? If that happens, we are thrown into a tailspin, feeling lost, out of control, without solid footing under us.

Let us look at a real example of how this might happen in life (with name and particulars changed to protect the individual). A man is a pillar of his community and of his church. Forty-two years of age, he is a genuinely solid person. He is not a hypocrite. He lives what he believes and is actually a role model for all those who know him. While not a saint, he is the kind of man every parent would like their son to be like some day.

One evening, while on a business trip to a distant city, he stops in a bar for a drink. For some reason, he consumes more than his usual limit of one drink. The alcohol causes him to let down his usually very solid guard. At this point, a woman who turns out to be a prostitute sits down next to him at the bar. Not knowing her occupation, he engages her in a conversation. The plot thickens when he senses an immediate instinctive attraction to this person. She begins to work her magic with her words and her hands. The next thing he knows, he is in a cheap hotel room having unprotected sex.

When he gets back to his own hotel room, he is devastated. In seventeen years of marriage, he has never once been unfaithful to his wife. In fact, he has never even put himself in such an uncompromising situation before. He cannot sleep. He is wracked with guilt. It is bad enough that he has broken his vows, but, in having unsafe sex, he now brings home the remote but real possibility that he is now infected with a venereal disease.

Such a man may have prayed before. In fact, he prays every night before he goes to bed and he never misses church on Sundays. I would suggest, however, that his prayer this day will look and feel different from any other prayer in his life. This prayer will come from his gut, from the soles of his feet, from every fiber in his being. It will have a note of urgency about it. He will feel, perhaps for the first time in his life, totally out of control. His defenses are down. If there was any smugness there before, it is gone now. Here is a man who is raw, who has been humbled. Here is a man ready for God.

Work Failure

I do not think that there is any culture in the world that places a higher premium on one's occupation than the United States of America. There are all kinds of reasons for this, but suffice it to say that it matters a lot to us what we do for a living.

It is not like this in other places in the world. For example, in Europe, when people meet you, they ask you two questions: 1) "What is your name?" and 2) "What things interest you in life?" In this country, the first question is the same, but the second question is, "What do you do for a living?" If people do not have something impressive to say when this question is asked, they frequently feel inferior.

People feel this way because – to put it bluntly – they are spiritually bankrupt. They feel like there is nothing inside them. Like performing seals, they are adept at jumping through hoops, but they do not know why they are doing so. They have become human "doings", not human "beings".

If someone is this shallow, this spiritually bankrupt, what happens to him if he loses his job? It can be absolutely devastating. It is as if such people do not know who they are anymore. They have become so identified with their job that they literally do not know who they are apart from the job. Take away the job, take away their identity.

What good could possibly emerge from this scenario? If this breakdown of all that they hold near and dear results in a breakthrough to their essence, then it can be a major turning point in life. It can result in a breakthrough back to the center of one's being. Or it can end up being just another missed chance at growth.

Let me give two scenarios: one that resulted in a lost opportunity for growth and one that resulted in a breakthrough. The opportunity happened when the man lost his job and proceeded to do two things that caused him to remain stuck or even to regress. First, he became bitter at life because this cruel twist of fate had him lose his job. And, second, he jumped at the first available job, even though he could have done much better had he looked around even a little bit. The real reason that he jumped at the first job that came along was that he simply could not bear to face his friends and tell them that he was out of work.

The person who lost a job and ended up growing as a result of the experience obviously handled it a lot differently. This individual saw the situation as a time to take a welcome rest, to step off the treadmill, to reassess her life, and look at the big picture. This new perspective resulted in a shift of priorities, more balance in life, and, most importantly, a spiritual breakthrough. With the forced leisure time on her hands, she chose to read some good spiritual literature and to try meditating. She came through this experience as a much fuller person. What could have been a breakdown going nowhere ended up being a breakthrough to the very center of her being.

Falling in Love

There are many forms of love. The ancient Greeks made all sorts of distinctions in this regard. They spoke about *eros* (erotic love), *ludus* (playful love), *agape* (spiritual love), and *storge* (friendship). All forms of love can lead us to a divine encounter. If "God is love" (St. John), then none of this should surprise us. But, in this chapter, we are talking about a thunderclap that can smash our defenses and cause the walls of Jericho to come tumbling down. For that experience, there is absolutely nothing like romantic love.

When Cupid comes calling, we are reduced to a temporary form of insanity. Being shot by one of Cupid's arrows can be a near-incapacitating experience. Even the toughest and the strongest find it all but impossible to resist. And that is why romantic love deserves to be included in this chapter: it breaks down the walls of the survival personality.

Cupid's arrival is seldom anticipated, but is never less welcome than when it arrives on the doorstep of one who is previously committed. Let's take an example. This example is from the movie Betrayal starring Jeremy Irons. In this plot, Irons plays the role of a calm, cool, and collected businessman, fabulously wealthy and successful. He is the kind of a man who never makes an uncalculated move. Supremely self-possessed, he is in control of every aspect of his life. At least he is until he meets his son's fianceé. Cupid strikes both him and the son's fianceé. About such matters, there is little choice. As they say, you don't choose love, it chooses you. Of course, other aspects of life enter in here like morality, commitments, etc. But, if a person is not reinforced by such things, and even when he or she *is* so reinforced, Cupid's attraction can be all but irresistible. In the movie, the liaison ends in tragedy, as such forbidden romances usually do, but the part that struck me was that the man was willing to risk absolutely everything for the sake of the attraction.

What are the implications of this for the spiritual path? Remember that loss of control is one of the essential parts of the spiritual journey. If that is the case, then romantic love can be an opportunity to experience powerlessness. It can then lead to a surrender to Higher Power with a deep reliance on something greater than ourselves.

Again, let us take a look at an example. A woman at work is smitten by her boss. The feeling is immediate and visceral. She feels herself blushing and perspiring and tripping over her words when she is in his presence. The situation is complicated by the fact that he seems to feel the same way about her. He takes her out to lunch. He buys her gifts. What we have here is a powder keg ready to explode. Ego energy is insufficient to contain this situation. The woman is aware that she is about to fall into a deep abyss that will be difficult to escape. The implications and the stakes are enormous. This is where Higher Power comes in. Unless she can humble herself and ask for help from a higher source, she is almost certain to fall.

That woman is in what is known as a crisis. The ancient Chinese have one character in their language for the word crisis, but it has two entirely different meanings. It means both danger as well as opportunity. It all depends on how things are handled. In our example, the woman may surrender totally to Cupid, in which case her life will invariably move in a totally new, and perhaps undesirable direction. Or perhaps the woman may admit her powerlessness, beseech help from a higher source, and survive the crisis more humble, wise and dependent upon Higher Power. If she goes the latter route, Cupid may have done her soul a favor when he shot her with one of his arrows.

War

All we have to do is to remember the images from the wars in Kosovo, Afghanistan and Iraq. Children terrified, women terrorized, and healthy young men reduced to the point of tears. That is the reality of war. One sees no arrogance, no swagger, no puffery, at least not among the innocent victims of war's aftermath. Some of the macho swagger is still on the faces of the untested soldiers, but think of the faces soldiers captured during combat. Beaten, humiliated, these young men and women now appear to be the picture of vulnerability.

War does that to people. It always has. It takes away all illusions of being safe, of being in control. And in that sense it can be another one of those teachable moments, those breakdowns of false pride leading to a breakthrough. Such breakthroughs do not happen automatically; but, let's put it this way, the odds of arrogance in a wartime situation are not real high.

Once again a story. My Dad was a tail gunner and a radioman on a TBF in the South Pacific during World War II. He never talked about his war experiences, never joined the VFW or the American Legion, never even bothered to pick up his Purple Heart that he earned when a shell hit his plane, shattering his flight glasses, and causing him partial disability in one of his eyes. All he wanted to do was to do his duty and then get home to his wife and baby son (me).

Many years later, his four children pumped him for information about his experiences. He talked about the experiences only reluctantly. Here are two of the stories that make the point of how vulnerable one can feel in wartime.

In one situation, their plane, a slow, lumbering, dive bomber, was unable to release a live bomb from the bay under the plane. They obviously could not land the plane that way. The pilot tried to shake the bomb loose but it would not release. The fuel gauge continued to drop. When they were just about ready to bail out of the plane in enemy territory, for some reason the bomb released on its own. My Dad said that every man on that plane had his heart in his throat and was saying his prayers. They thought they were going to die that day.

The other story he told us that I never forgot was the time his plane was hit and one of the wheels was shot off. They were going to have to land on one wheel. The pilot told the other two men, "As soon as we come to a stop, run for your lives." With sparks flying everywhere, my Dad sprinted out of that plane faster than he has ever run before or since.

Here is the point. Can you imagine any of the men in that plane being smug and arrogant? No way. The sheer vulnerability of combat humbles people. Preparation for combat does that to warriors. And it goes without saying that the non-combatants are terrified beyond all belief.

A number of years ago, I did a series of programs for U.S. Army chaplains around the world. One hears a lot about Generation X, with their post-religious attitudes about life. Well, there must be something about military life that restores post-religious thinking to its religious mindset. One of the chaplains told me that young men and women in the military are still generally very religious. Maybe it has to do with being in harm's way, even during training missions. But the bottom line is that thoughts of God are often very much part of the picture. The chaplain gave me an example. He said if he is handing out medallions to the Catholic personnel, *everyone* gets in line for one. It is almost as if the soldiers are saying, "I will take all the help I can get."

Now, granted, there is nothing very sophisticated about any of this. Much of it boils down to forms of superstition. Very little has been thought through. But not all of life happens in the head. These kinds of visceral experiences change people in deep ways as much as anything else does. We have all heard the expression, "There are no atheists in foxholes." There is a lot of truth to that statement. At least for the time when one is in the foxhole, all pretense of being in control vanishes.

Two images from the movies come to mind. In the movie <u>Saving Private Ryan</u> (widely regarded as the most realistic war movie ever made), one of the young men on the landing craft kisses the crucifix around his neck as his boat gets ready to hit the beach. Later in the movie, the sharpshooter quotes a psalm as he fires his machine gun from a tower at a Nazi convoy. This admixture of religion and war is not as strange as it may seem at first. And it is not strange at all to those who have been in combat. War humbles the proud, a necessary precondition to a right relationship with Higher Power. It is a path that not all that many can relate to from first hand experience, but it is a path that has changed some people for the rest of their lives. It deserves to be mentioned here.

Sickness and Dying

While relatively few people can relate to combat experiences, absolutely everyone can relate to sickness, aging, and dying. It is a central experience of the human condition. Everyone must deal with all three experiences eventually. Of course, the young seem relatively "immune" from these things at first, but it is only a matter of time for them. They will have to deal with it eventually.

As people move into mid-life, all of this becomes much more real. One of the first and most dramatic ways of dealing with the aging process has to do with going through it vicariously with our parents. There is a saying that you have not really grown up in life until you have buried both of your parents. As long as at least one parent is alive, people report that they still feel to some extent like a child. But, when both parents have died, there is a kind of passing of the baton from one generation to another. The surviving child now feels like an adult, fully responsible for one's life.

As the transitory nature of life presents itself, people also come face to face with the existential question: "Where are my parents now? Where will I be when I die?" There are really only two possible answers to those questions. Answer number one is that, despite the pain and the incongruities of life, somehow it all holds together. Death is not the end. There is meaning in life. It can be trusted. It is worth living. The second answer comes from Shakespeare who has one of his characters, Macbeth, say, "Life is a tale told by an idiot, full of sound and fury, signifying nothing." There really is no middle ground. Either it all makes sense or none of it does. Since spirituality is all about meaning, the existential questions about life and death offer us a chance for a quantum leap forward spiritually, if we can surrender to the fact that all of life, including death, is full of meaning.

Of course, it becomes particularly difficult to deal with death if we are dealing with the death of a child, especially our own child. At least with the death of our parents, we have some sense that this is the natural order of things: the old die before the young. But what do we do when we must face the death of a child? In my experience, this is the ultimate personal tragedy, the ultimate testing that any adult can undergo. There are no easy answers here. One cannot reason oneself to inner peace about this topic. There are too many incongruities, too much that does not feel right. Only surrender to a larger plan that we will never be able to see can extricate our troubled spirits from this morass in which we find ourselves. Such a scenario will humble even the toughest individual. What do we do when we find out that our child is dying from leukemia or some other life-threatening disease? We do what we can to get help for the disease, but then we must put it all in the hands of someone or something that is greater and smarter and more powerful than us. There is no other way.

And what about our *own* aging and dying? It is a truism that life passes very quickly. We are young and invulnerable, seeming to have life by the tail, and then one day we either get a report from our doctor that we do not want to hear or we take a look in the mirror and we are shocked by what we see.

I can remember my first real wake-up call in life. I dutifully went in for my annual checkup just because I have always been a good boy and did what I was told. But I knew it would be a waste of time, because I have perfect health. Imagine my shock when the doctor found a basal cell on my neck. A minor skin cancer, nothing to worry about. However, when you are young and seemingly invulnerable, you do not even expect to hear your name and cancer mentioned in the same sentence. Since then, I have had a few suspicious growths removed and I watched my uncle die of melanoma.

These are the kinds of things that get our attention in life. They can put us in crisis. Once again, we can go in either of two ways. If we handle things poorly, we will say that, since I am getting older, maybe I should try to recapture my youth before it is too late. This may lead to something like: 1) heavy duty cosmetic surgery; 2) having an affair with someone younger than us; 3) buying a sportscar; 4) moving to the "right" place; or 5) quitting our job before having thought through the decision. If we deal with our situation in the best way possible, however, we will look at our aging bodies and choose to identify with the consciousness of which the body is only the vehicle. When this happens, we can actually surrender to the aging process as a part of life. Of course, if we think that we are the same thing as our bodies, then we will think that *we* are dying. But, if we can die to this exclusive identification with the body, then we have already begun to experience eternal life. As the expression goes, "The person who dies before they die, does not die when they die." In other words, when we can learn to disidentify from an exclusive identification with our bodies when we are alive, and when we can disidentify from that survival personality that we have talked about so much, then we have *already* begun to enter eternity.

Jesus put it this way, "Unless a person dies to him (or her) self, he (or she) cannot enter eternal life." This has nothing to do with some form of masochistic self-hatred. What Jesus is trying to tell us is that we are more than our bodies, more than our minds, more than our emotions, more than our education, or our bank accounts, or our jobs, or even our relationships. Each one of us is, in essence, Christ. When we can let go of all of these partial identifications, we will be able to live in freedom, peace, joy, and love. Sickness, aging, and death all conspire to break down the belief that we are nothing more than our bodies. They help to make possible the breakthrough into spirit that is our birthright.

Something More

One of the most common forms of breakdown is the hardest one of all to define. It has to do with a breaking down of all of our illusions of the things we thought would make us really happy in life. A spiritual traveler finds at the end of the journey that there is this incredible disconnect between what society says is the source of happiness and what experience eventually shows us.

To put it simply, society tells us that "it" is "out there". Not knowing any differently, we plunge merrily "out there" in search of "it". What we find, after a lifetime of searching, is that all of those things "out there", when eventually acquired, end up tasting like sawdust in our mouths.

Madison Avenue is a multi-billion dollar industry set up to tell us what we need. Here are some of the essentials: 1) an ever-young, ever-sexy mate; 2) a luxury car; 3) a gorgeous home; 4) designer clothes; 4) alluring perfumes and colognes; 5) the right vodka; and 6) priceless antiques.

Honestly, truly, I have nothing against any of those things. In fact, I would like some of those things! But this much I have learned after 59 years of life: none of those things will ever bring me or anyone else inner peace and joy. What we are all looking for comes from within, never from without. This is a law, not a rule. It is just the way things really are in life.

Proving that the psyche is truly ingenious at trying to have its cake and eat it too, a new industry has arisen in our day: the spirituality business. In a typically American approach, you can attend a weekend workshop and try to "get" spirituality. There, in a downtown hotel, are five or six of the people who "really know". Just pay them big bucks and they will tell you what you will need to know and then you can go home on Sunday, having gotten "it", and be ready to be at work on Monday morning without missing a beat. The whole thing is cynical and sickening.

I must confess that, being considered by some to be an expert in spirituality (after all, I have an M.A. in spirituality to "prove" it!), that I make a living by being a mentor and a teacher, helping people to grow spiritually. But here is the important point. I do not have anything that anyone else does not have. I cannot give someone something that they already have. I would be doing a disservice to people to try to pass myself off as a guru. Guru is spelled, "Gee, you are you". Those who soak up the projections of others, and bask in the transferences, are doing their clients a disservice and, they will eventually discover, doing themselves a disservice as well.

No, we cannot find the truth *anywhere* out there. But, before we can really appreciate this truth, we often have to exhaust ourselves in an outer search. We "get" the beautiful mate, the flashy car, and all of the other things that are supposed to do it for us. We might even "have" the latest spiritual teacher in our bag of tricks. But then it all begins to break down. The mate gets wrinkles and is eventually affected by gravity. The same thing happens to our second or third partner. Our luxury car looks good, but we notice that it does not take away our inner pain. The vodka can only make us high for so long. And, if we find out that our spiritual teacher has secretly become a millionaire and is sleeping with his or her disciples, we become disillusioned there too. It is at this point that we ask ourselves the question that the singer, Patti Page asked in a song, "Is that all there is?"

I believe that this stage is a wonderful one for us to attain. I am all for disillusionment and disenchantment. Think of the origin of those two words. An illusionist is a magician. When we become disillusioned, this means that we have begun to see what is really going on behind the magic tricks. Like Dorothy, we pull away the curtain and see that there is no wizard after all. He is, instead, someone who is "a very good man, just not a very good wizard," as the Wizard said of himself when Toto exposed him. All of these things and persons that we have pursued are all good; but they are just not God.

An enchanter is someone who casts a spell. Many of us, perhaps most of us, have been under a spell since childhood. Parents, teachers, clergy, all pointed us outside of ourselves. We believed them. Follow the rules, be a good citizen, make a lot of money, go to church every week. This was the formula for success. We followed it, so why are we not happy? Asking that question is the beginning of healing.

When someone tells me they are disenchanted, I always think to myself, "Great!" Now maybe some healing can take place. The spell, the enchantment, the brainwashing is over. The person now at least realizes what does *not* work. Now we can get somewhere.

All of this disillusionment and disenchantment, this disgust with various things as a substitute for a spiritual hunger and thirst, is actually a breaking down of false idols. Doesn't one of the commandments have something to say about not making false idols? It is based upon the deep truth that putting ones absolute trust in any one thing or person or system is disempowering to the human person. It is alienating and fragmenting. It takes us away from where we need to go, and that is ultimately deep within our soul.

Life is ingenious at getting our attention. Just as our dreams are unique to us alone, life seems to choose just the right crisis for us in order to tear down our resistances. Although it does not feel like it, the tearing down process is a great favor to us. We recognize this, however, only in retrospect. The summer of 1976, when I went through the toughest part of my spiritual crisis, was, simultaneously, the best of times and the worst of times for me. On one hand, I suffered such psychological pain that I considered suicide. On the other hand, whatever freedom and creativity that I experienced today can be traced back by me to that summer of my discontent.

The reason that the pain was all worth it to me, and the reason that the spiritual journey is worth the pain to any of us, is that the breakdown of the survival personality enables us to experience our natural self, our true self, our divine self. As pastoral counselors, we need to embrace the holiness of the breakdowns if we are ever to hope for authentic breakthroughs.

Who or what is this self that lies within us? What is the difference between the ego, the survival personality, and our true self? This will be the topic of our next chapter. This is not just a case of semantics. What is being referred to here are states of consciousness that can imprison us in an inner hell or set us free to soar with eagle's wings.

IV. Discovering the Authentic Self

CHAPTER TEN

The Self Behind the Ego

In Chapter Two, we elaborated at some length on the role of the ego on the spiritual path. But is the ego the king or queen of the psyche? Not exactly. The ego is accountable to what Jung called the Self. While it may seem as if we are just quibbling with words here, that is not the case. These distinctions are important to the purpose of this book: explaining as clearly as possible what is involved in growing spiritually and living an authentic life.

It is true that words are only sounds and symbols and not a substitute for the experience of living. But words are powerful. They help us shape our worldview. Look at how feminism has made us conscious of how important inclusive language is. So making this distinction between the Self and the ego is an important challenge.

Jung had a simple distinction that he made between the Self and the ego. He called the Self the "big self" and the ego the "little self". For him, the Self refers to our consciousness as being not just a little skin-encapsulated creature, but as the earth being conscious of itself through you and me. The ego is not a separate creature; it is just a very narrow, very focused, laser-like application of universal consciousness to the here-and-now.

John Firman and Ann Russell, whom I mentioned earlier as psychosynthesist scholars, say that the Self is the deeper ontological reality of which the ego, or "I", is a reflection.[8] They and Jung agree with one another; they just use different words to make their point.

Which part of us should be in charge? On one level, it is the ego that should be running the show. But the job of the ego is to function kind of like the CEO of the psyche. It is to call all the shots, to run the show, but *only after taking orders from the True Self.* If the ego were not so wounded, this would not be a problem. The ego would report for duty every day, just like a good soldier, and ask how it might serve the True Self. But remember what the problem is here: we can no longer even access the pure ego, because this hybrid creature - the survival personality - is trying to be in charge. The survival personality is not even aware of being in conflict with the ego. What it has done is that is has usurped the throne of the ego. It does not even know that the ego, the sacred child, even exists anymore.

As we have seen in Chapter Three, the survival personality has no independent existence in itself. It is a fear-based construct, utterly without any permanence in being. It is a house of cards waiting to collapse as soon as the ego, the sacred child within, can manifest itself again.

If it is true that the survival personality has no independent existence in itself, the same can be said of the ego, the sacred child within. The sacred child exists as a reflection from the mirror of Ultimate Reality.

When we look into a mirror, we see ourselves, but this is actually only a reflection of ourselves. In the same way, all of creation is a mirror image of Ultimate Reality. Even on the level of our sacred child, we have no independent existence. Our forms and even our psyches spring out of the void – a mysterious condition, often called God, or True

Self, or Source, from which creation arises – and one day will return to it. In the meantime, we live in the world of form, but it is form that is never permanent. We are made in the image and likeness of the True Self; but we are not the True Self in the sense of being the creator of the world.

The consciousness of being the sacred child is called "Christ consciousness", or "Buddha consciousness." We represent the second polarity of divinity, the created pole. The sacred child knows that he or she is at one with the Divine, charged with spirit, with no independent existence apart from the Source. We creatures in form represent, in religious terms, the embodied presence of God.

The spiritually evolved person is the one who recognizes the sacred presence in all things. This is not to say that we all have a drop of the divine within us. Rather *every part of us* is ultimately divine in nature. All teachings to the contrary are falsehoods. Our bodies, our lives - even when dysfunctional or mired in addiction - all participate in the divine process, the divine dance. It is just that our spiritual blindness often causes us to feel cut off, separate, and filled with guilt.

What we need when we feel cut off from our True Self is what psychologist William James calls a "cleansing of the doors of perception." We need to dispel the lie of separation and realize that we are and always will be divine beings.

Is there a danger in claiming our divine birthright? Of course. It is what Carl Jung calls "inflation," allowing our egos to become inflated with the archetype of the Self. People who have become possessed by this archetype can – like David Koresh at the Waco, Texas religious community which burned up at the end of a long siege by lawmen – look us straight in the eye and tell us that they are Jesus Christ. And, in a sense they are. But, they are also the devil and the hero and all of the other primordial spiritual energies in the psyche. The trick is to identify with the archetype of the Christ and then to disidentify from it. We *have* it, but we are *not* it. We *carry* divinity; we do not generate it.

This is what the perennial philosophy and psychology have tried to communicate over the centuries: that we are all divine beings, but that our consciousness either runs away from this truth or becomes possessed by it. The "I am" consciousness of Jesus, the Buddha, and all self-realized beings, is that "The Father and I are one," (John 10:30) not on the level of ontology, but on the level of full participation. It is this consciousness to which all of us are evolving.

Spiritual psychology insists on holding people in this larger context. It sees the ego and the body as charged with spirit, yet it recognizes the fact that the spiritual journey is all about uncovering this forgotten truth about who we are. The truth is not a new one, and the journey is not even really a journey at all. It is just a waking up to who we have always been but have forgotten that we are: divine beings. As the poet T.S. Eliot puts it in the lovely mystical poem _Four Quartets_, "And the end of all our exploring will be to arrive where we started and know the place for the first time."

The True Self

Who or what is this Self or True Self and how is it different from the ego and the survival personality? Actually, they are all interrelated, but they represent very different states of consciousness of the individual. Let's look at it this way:

Survival Personality	Ego	True Self
(Wounded)	(Healthy)	(Fully Evolved)

We have already examined the survival personality. This is the fear-based state of consciousness of most people most of the time. It is characterized by feelings of shame, insufficiency, lack, and low self-esteem.

A healthy functioning person on the other hand, has a healthy ego. This person has, more often than not, feelings of positive self-regard, self-acceptance, and self-esteem. This individual is self-actualized, a self-starter, able to contribute positively to society. You have probably noticed the word "self" mentioned here a lot. This is because a healthy functioning ego is considered the end-point of development by most psychologies. Certainly that is the case with most Freudians. The whole goal is to lessen suffering by the individual through lessening the impact of the Id and the Superego in everyday life. A noble goal, to be sure. Certainly a fear-based individual would long for this state of consciousness.

Other schools of counseling each have their own unique ways of looking at the human person. Each school has something to offer; each makes a positive contribution to our understanding of the human person. Besides the psychoanalytic theory (Freud), there are all sorts of other perspectives: Adlerian, existential, person-centered, gestalt, reality therapy, family systems, etc. But none of these schools are able to account for the highest states of consciousness reported universally by spiritual journeyers over the centuries,.

The Behaviorists, whether the classical types of B.F. Skinner, or more modern versions like the Cognitive Behaviorists, have even less interest in the human psyche than the above mentioned schools. Their stated purpose is very clear and unambiguous: change people's behavior. All else is irrelevant.

None of the more common schools of psychology have much meaningful to say at all about states of higher consciousness reported by millions of spiritual seekers. Only the transpersonal school and integral school of psychology deal with this in any substantial manner.

Here we run into a bit of a snag. While millions have reported this state of consciousness, there is absolutely no consensus on what to call it. Here are some of the more common names for this state of consciousness:

- The True Self (used by Thomas Merton)

- The Self (used by Carl Jung)

- The Inner Core

- Ones Essential Self

- The God Self

- The Christ Self

- The Divine Spark

- Atman (in Hinduism)

- Adonai (Jewish mysticism)

- One's Core Self

- Spirit

- Soul

The snag referred to comes from a thing called "ineffability". What this means is that the experience is one thing; your interpretation of the experience is something else entirely. It is hard, in other words, to adequately describe something that is, by definition, beyond words.

A story illustrates this well. The noted Trappist monk Thomas Merton made a trip to Southeast Asia from his monastery in Kentucky. (He died suddenly and mysteriously while on his journey.) Merton met a famous Buddhist monk and it is reported that the two of them spent a period of meditation together. When they opened their eyes, they looked at one another and were sure that they had contacted the same reality and attained the same level of consciousness. So far so good. But then they began to discuss their experience, and that is where they began to disagree. Their experience was being filtered through the left brain, and there their egos and belief systems came into play and they could reach no consensus. So, in other words, one's experience and one's interpretation of the experience are two different things entirely.

Wars have been fought over whose definitions are correct. So I will not be so naïve as to say that one term is the best one or even to suggest that the terms are culturally relative. What I would suggest, however, is that we could, perhaps, agree on a description of this state of consciousness. Even here, we may run into some problems, but there is a better chance, I think, of finding a consensus.

In our final chapter, we will describe at length what these higher states of consciousness look like. But let's not put the cart before the horse. Before we move into our inner heaven, we need to come to terms with a very important part of spiritual growth: forgiveness. This might not seem, at first glance, to be all that crucial to our task at hand, but we simply cannot go forward spiritually until we address this aspect of life. All of the spiritual traditions are in agreement on this fact, so let us deal with it in our next chapter.

CHAPTER ELEVEN

Forgiveness

Forgiveness is essential to spiritual growth. All spiritual teachers and traditions agree on this. However, distortions about what forgiveness means, and what it does not mean, have actually contributed to needless suffering for many spiritual seekers. The purpose of this chapter will be to cast some light on this very important topic, and set the record straight as to what should be the appropriate approach to this attitude, which is so crucial for our spiritual growth.

First of all, let us make something clear. Forgiveness comes *after* you have processed whatever you are feeling. This point needs to be made right now. That is because spiritual types (or guilt-ridden religious types) frequently tend to short-circuit the forgiveness process by skipping over their feelings. This inevitably backfires and leads to all sorts of problems.

As usual, let us look at an example, albeit a rather extreme one. A young woman in her twenties finally musters up the courage to begin dealing with the fact that her older brother sexually abused her on a regular basis when she was just a child. Naturally she is overwhelmed by feelings of

147

anger and outrage toward her brother. Yet she does not wish to burn all bridges in her relationship with her now adult brother. She is truly in a quandary as to what to do.

This is the time for some skillful psychotherapy. The anger must be dealt with in a safe way. Issues like proper boundaries, assertiveness, etc. must be explored. But let us, for the sake of argument, say that the young woman belongs to a strong, fundamentalist Christian church that holds a lot of influence over her. It is possible that she might have a pastor who urges her to forgive her brother immediately. The pastor takes several quotes from scripture out of context as a way of buttressing his or her point of view.

Now the young woman's dilemma is even more pronounced. Now the big guns of religion have been hauled out. Now she feels that she must forgive her brother immediately or be considered a bad person.

While the example of sexual abuse by one's brother may be an extreme (although by no means unheard of) example, the advice that she is given in this instance is by no means atypical. I have seen it happen hundreds of times. Well-meaning religious types speak constantly about forgiveness. Fair enough. Forgiveness is crucial to spiritual growth. That is the overall point of this chapter, but the forgiveness needs to take place *after* the person has had an adequate amount of time to deal with their feelings. The emotional processing is essential for authenticity of the self.

If processing our feelings is so important, how much time should we allow for people to accomplish this? The answer is: as long as it takes. Sometimes a client can work things through in a few weeks. Sometimes the process can take years. A therapist (even one with an expressly Christian perspective) must not try to hurry along the process. It must be assumed that the person needs to hold on to their anger for the protection of their psyche, if they are at this time unable to forgive. Pushing them too fast in this regard can actually reverse the person's recovery.

Once again, I have seen for myself the damage that can happen when people feel constrained by religious scruples to forgive immediately. As the chapter on depression points out, undealt with anger frequently goes underground (i.e. in the unconscious) and usually ends up in a major depression.

The examples I have given so far have had to do with Christianity. This is for a good reason. No other religion emphasizes forgiveness to the extent that Christianity does. Judaism, for example, emphasizes justice over forgiveness. It speaks of "an eye for an eye, a tooth for a tooth." Islam preaches the value of the *jihad*, the holy war. This is certainly not to imply that mercy and forgiveness are not advocated in Judaism and Islam. Clearly they are. It is just a matter of emphasis. Christianity makes forgiveness a linchpin of its philosophy. Because it is so central to its beliefs, it is easy, I think, to see how easily it can be misunderstood.

Religion is not the only culprit here. Certain New Age systems of thought tend to short-circuit the legitimate place of "negative" feelings as well. If you look at brochures from many weekend workshops, there is lots of talk about love and light and transcendence of the limitations of the body, and very little on dealing with one's legitimate feelings. In particular, I would single out <u>A Course in Miracles</u> for some soul-searching in this regard.

First of all, let me say that I have the greatest respect for <u>A Course in Miracles</u>, which is a spiritual text whose authorship is attributed to Jesus. I have studied it since 1976 and have seen its positive influence on hundreds of people. Also, when it is properly understood and nuanced, I have no problem with it whatsoever. It is just that it is so easy to distort. An inexperienced teacher could easily emphasize not judging others to the point where a person could feel guilty if they still react in an angry manner in certain situations. Once again, I have seen skillful leaders handle this properly. But, in my role as a spiritual counselor, I have encountered many people who have been confused by all this. It often seems to them like a warmed over version of the old axiom that spiritual people do not get angry. Well, in point of fact, spiritual people *do* get angry. Hopefully, the chapter dealing with anger made this point abundantly clear.

The Importance of Forgiveness

Having established the danger of premature forgiveness, let me now make something crystal clear: without forgiveness, there can be no spiritual growth. Why? Is it because of some rule that someone has laid down? No. It is not about rules at all. It is about laws. The law being referred to is this: when we condemn and judge others, we do the same to ourselves. When we forgive others, we forgive ourselves.

The issue has to do with the oneness of all things. We feel most in harmony with life when we manifest love to all parts of life. When we close off love to even one part of life, we begin to shut down our sense of connectedness to all things. This brings about pain and suffering and a sense of alienation in our lives.

Forgiving others, or, rather, refusing to judge people in the first place, is a classical win/win attitude in life. First of all, when we refrain from judging others, we win. We feel inner peace and harmony with all creatures. We hold fast to a state of consciousness that can only be described as being "in love" with all beings. Such a state of consciousness brings blessings to us on a number of levels. Without the stress, without the constant adrenaline flow, our body is healthier. Without the obsessive thoughts centering around hurt and revenge, we can think in a more clear and free way. Without the energy drain involved in seeing others as the enemy, we are able to be more creative in life.

The other side of the equation is that others benefit by our non-judgmental ways as well. Einstein has established the absolute interconnectedness of all things with his unified field theory. The idea that we can have our own private hate and revenge is an illusion. "Whatever you bind on earth shall be considered bound in heaven; whatever you loose on earth shall be considered loosed in heaven". (Matt 16:19) These words were not just intended for Saint Peter. They are a teaching to all of humanity that we have the power to imprison people or set them free by the thoughts and feelings that we hold toward them. On one level, people can "feel" our lack of forgiveness or our own blessing toward them, even if they are thousands of miles away from us. We hold it within our power to keep people imprisoned or to set them free. (See Figure 13)

An example from my own life comes to mind. One pastor I worked with always seemed to rub me the wrong way and vice versa. One day, I went through an experience that changed the dynamics of the relationship. The change had nothing to do with working things out with the pastor. It had to do with working things out within myself. I was at an Intensive Journal workshop led by a trainee of psychologist Ira Progoff. We were to simply put ourselves totally in the shoes of someone with whom we were having difficulties. We were to feel things as they felt them, to imagine - based on what we knew about them - what it was like to grow up in the family that produced them. We were to try to put ourselves in their place and time, and to imagine how they felt inside.

When the experience was over, I was in tears. I could truly feel this man's pain. I now "knew" why he reacted to me the way he did. It all made perfect sense to me. From that day forward, our relationship changed. I never said a word to him about my experience. I simply began to treat him in a different way, based upon the compassion that I now felt for him. He responded in kind. The healing had taken place, and it had all happened from within. It all had to do with withdrawing my judgments and condemnations about him. I had set him free by my refusal to judge him anymore, and, in the process, I had set myself free.

Forgiveness

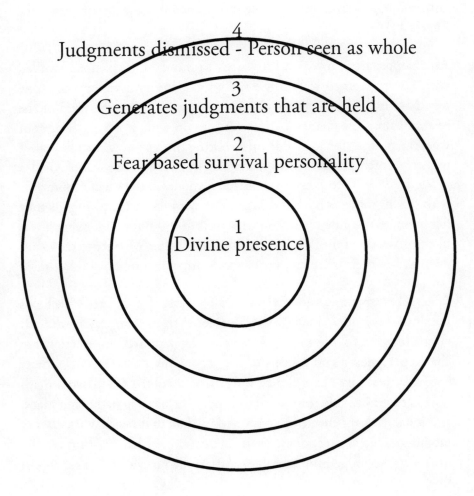

Figure Thirteen

When Forgiveness Fails

The above personal story is a success story. Now I want to share a story where the forgiveness did not "take." This is the other side of the coin. In this instance, while we may set someone free from within, for reasons known only to God total reconciliation simply does not happen.

This is the story of another pastor with whom I served. Yes, I know, it looks like I may have had authority issues in my youth. That is certainly true. For pastors from the old school, I was a real challenge. Radical, untraditional, not buying into the clerical subculture, I must have pushed every one of their buttons. Of course, they pushed my buttons as well. We were shadows of one another. They were everything that I never wanted to be; I represented to them everything that was wrong in a changing church.

In any event, in one particularly volatile relationship, an attempt was made to systematically destroy me on every level of my being. Within six weeks, I was trying to get a transfer. I was gone within six months. Such a short period of time, but such pain, such scarring. After dealing with my feelings of hurt, I began the process of forgiveness. I was able to forgive, to eventually eliminate all conscious feelings of resentment, but I noticed something very telling about what happened next. I noticed that, whenever I was in the presence of the person who tried to destroy me, I began to perspire and tense up. This tells me that my forgiveness apparently was not and is not complete. The body never lies. With those kinds of physical reactions, my body was telling me something. It was telling me that I am apparently still holding onto something.

When this happens, when we are unable to forgive someone totally, then what do we do? It seems to me that the life of Jesus gives us a clue here. I am referring specifically to his being nailed to the cross. He says the words that we have all heard, "Father, forgive them; they do not know what they are doing." (Luke 23:34) Of particular note here is the fact that Jesus does not say, "I forgive you." His human side was hurting too much for him to do that. So he turned to Higher Power

153

within himself, the same Higher Power that is within us, and said, so to speak, "O.K. God, you will have to forgive them on this one. I just can't do it myself right now."

Sometimes that is the best that we can do. We give it our best shot. We eliminate all of the hatred that might be in our hearts. At least that much has to happen in order for us to keep growing spiritually. But we might conceivably reach an impasse, a roadblock. At that point, we need to turn it over to the God within us to do the forgiving. For we recognize that, at least for now, we can do no more.

This decision must be reached with a level of self-forgiveness as well. Forgiveness is not denial ("I haven't done anything wrong"), nor is it rationalization ("What I have done wrong isn't all that bad after all"). True forgiveness of self is a gift we give ourselves, based on the realization in our inner consciousness that we are forgiven by the universe for all of our "sins".

The word for "sin" in the Christian scriptures is *amartia*, which means "missing the mark". There is no judgment implied, certainly no guilt trip required. It is simply the acknowledgment that, just as an archer does not always hit a bulls eye, we do not always get it right either. "Right," of course, means to be centered in God. We can forgive ourselves with the realization that, in life, no one bats .1000. That is why they put erasers on pencils. We are beings "in process", learning by our mistakes, loved by the Source exactly as we are. If this is the case, we certainly have permission to love and forgive ourselves as well. We are under no divine mandate to judge ourselves or others. In fact, just the opposite is true. We are to hold no judgments and to be absolutely prodigal (excessive) in our forgiveness of self and one another.

However, are we not letting ourselves off the hook a little too easily here? What about Jesus' injunction that we are to "be perfect as our heavenly father is perfect"? (Matt 6:48) There is perhaps no other line in Scripture that is more frequently misunderstood than this one. In order to understand what it means, we must look at its total context.

Jesus has just finished telling his disciples a story. It is all about the indiscriminate nature of God's love. To make his point about the generosity of God's love, Jesus gives the example of the blessings of the rainfall. He says that his father allows "his rain to fall on honest and dishonest men alike." (Matt 6:45) He then goes on to say the line about being perfect as God is perfect. What is going on here? What is the connection between the story and its conclusion? It has to do with the word for "perfect" in Aramaic, the language Jesus spoke. The word does not imply being without flaw or blemish. It has to do with being generous and all-inclusive. The sense of the teaching, then, is this: God is not stingy with blessings. Everyone gets them, whether they deserve them or not. You must be the same way. Accept every part of yourself, without distinction. Accept even your weaknesses. If you do, you will be "perfect" in the sense that Jesus means it.

Forgiving the Unforgivable

Inevitably, the objection is raised: what about those people who apparently are really evil; are we to forgive them as well? What about the Hitlers and the Stalins of the world? Are we supposed to forgive these people as well? Why should I? There seems to be no good in them at all. These are apparently dangerous, evil people.

At this point, an important distinction needs to be made. While it is in everyone's best interest to forgive others, that does not mean that we are to approve of their actions. Their actions, if evil, deserve to be condemned and actively opposed. It is not unspiritual to protect the innocent. It is not unspiritual to use some common sense and to protect the world from acts of destruction.

Let us take a real life example: the mass killer Charles Manson. To develop spiritually, the challenge is to love him as a human being. He is one of God's children, too. His essence is divine. Nothing that he ever does will ever be able to extinguish the divine spark within him. If we hate him, we become less than fully human. But, while all this is true, it is also true that he is very dangerous. I, for one, do not want him walking amidst society. He, like Hitler, was physically abused as a boy. His mother was a prostitute who used to service men in front of her son. These facts help me to understand Charles Manson. But it would be insanity to conclude that spiritual love invites self-destructive decisions. No, Charles Manson deserves to be right where he is, locked away in a maximum security prison.

Of course, anything is possible. People can change. After all, that was why the Quakers called prisons penitentiaries. They were seen as places where people could repent and then change. Even the idea of solitary confinement had a spiritual origin. The theory was that, being alone – with only a Bible to read – a person could conceivably see the error of their ways and then change. While this theory still holds water, only a naive optimist would conclude that there is a likelihood that a Charles Manson could change that way. In life, sometimes the patterns that set in are so deep that, barring a miracle, the person is incapable of any meaningful change.

An analogy could be made to the progression of a disease such as cancer. If it is caught early enough, there is a good prognosis for a cure. If, however, it is not detected until its advanced stages, it is unlikely that modern science, or even some manifestation of faith healing, could do anything about it. In the same way, if a psychologically or spiritually sick individual is caught early enough in life, perhaps something can be done. But, if their deterioration is too far along, there is not much that can be done by anyone.

The above examples of Hitler, Stalin, and Manson, all have to do with public figures. But how do we handle the forgiveness issue if we have been severely wounded by someone in our own life? Again, let us take an example so that we do not get too abstract. How would a man be expected to act if he is trying to come to terms with being sexually abused by a teacher, a Scout master, a clergyperson, or some other trusted figure? I chose this example because these types of betrayals by authority figures are among the most difficult ones to handle.

First of all, let the rage and the outrage be felt fully for as long as it takes. This could best be handled in the safe container of a therapeutic context. Second, in order to feel fully safe and secure, the individual should not feel guilty about bringing in the law, if that is appropriate. If the law is not there to protect the innocent, then who is it there to protect? Such a public ordeal may be too much for the individual to handle. That would be a personal call to make. Finally, however, after all of the above steps, it is incumbent upon the wronged individual to try to forgive his or her perpetrator.

We need a word of caution here. Forgiving someone does not mean rationalizing away the horrible nature of the crime. It does not mean minimizing the impact that the abuse had. But it does mean letting go of the hate and the resentment. Why? Because, if we do not let go of the venom, it will back up on us and poison us.

When Jesus, in particular, and other spiritual teachers as well, tell us to forgive seventy times seven, they are telling us what we need to do to attain serenity and inner peace. We are not dealing with a should, an ought, or some other injunction. We are dealing with the wisdom of the ages. It is one thing to be a beautiful person who is temporarily angry. It is another thing entirely to be an angry person. Angry people will never inherit the kingdom of heaven. This is another way of saying that, when we are holding on to anger, when we have swallowed it and let it become a part of us, then we are in a state of dis-ease. In such a state, it is very difficult, if not impossible, to feel tuned into our spiritual essence.

I hope it has become very clear in this chapter that forgiveness is a process that must not be hurried along. It is not a trivial matter. But it is also true that life can feel wonderful when we have reconciled things at least within our own hearts. Life is too short as it is. Every day spent dwelling with hatred is one less day without serenity.

Forgiveness of others is, then, crucial to our spiritual growth. But it is just as crucial – perhaps even more so – for us to learn how to forgive ourselves. This is not an easy thing to do for most of us, especially if we are talking about forgiving ourselves for weaknesses and shortcomings that just won't go away. These parts of us are deeply embarrassing to us. We wish they weren't there. We do our best to banish these parts into our unconscious. But it never works. The self-forgiveness is simply never complete until we surface all of these ghosts and goblins from within and learn to come to terms with them. It is now time for us to deal with how the spiritual journeyer can come to terms with the darkness within us all.

CHAPTER TWELVE

The Shadow Knows

It is one thing to forgive others for being imperfect; it is something else entirely to forgive ourselves. For some reason, the latter is often more difficult than the former. Forgiving ourselves entails, first of all, facing ourselves. Maybe that is why self-acceptance is so difficult. There is just so much within us that embarrasses us and repulses us.

Somewhere along the way we picked up some unrealistic ideas about being perfect. We often have it wired in our heads that we cannot forgive ourselves until we have it "all together." Let us make this point crystal clear: we are *never* going to get it "all together" as long as we are alive. Can we then still bring ourselves to forgive ourselves, even though we will *always* be less than perfect?

This chapter deals with the crucial question of how spiritual growth is compatible with human imperfection. This is an area often overlooked or glossed over in books on spirituality. All human beings are and always will be flawed. What are the implications of this humbling truth for us spiritual journeyers?

Besides having a false self (the survival personality) and a true self (our divine essence), we also have an idealized self. This is the image of ourselves that we would <u>like</u> to be and that we would like to appear to be to others. So far so good. There is nothing wrong about having ideals and wishing to live according to those ideals.

But what do we do with the parts of ourselves that do not correspond to the ideal that we have of ourselves? What do we do with all of those dimensions of ourselves that we have judged to be shameful or unworthy or just personally undesirable and distasteful? We bury them deep within our unconscious.

Of course, very little of this is done consciously. It is as if when we strive to identify exclusively with only ideal parts of ourselves, the rest of us just "falls" into the unconscious and disappears. All of this material, what we judge to be unworthy of us or the part of ourselves that we never allow ourselves to embrace, becomes our shadow.

Because we are afraid of the dark and of the unknown, we often tend to attach ominous overtones to the shadow. But there is absolutely nothing inherently evil or unworthy about the shadow. It is just the part of ourselves that does not jibe with our persona, the image that we project to the world. (See Figure 14)

The only problem with relegating our shadow to the unconscious is that, while it may disappear, it does not dissolve. It now functions as a semi-autonomous force within us that demands recognition. If we eventually find a way to acknowledge and embrace the shadow, of course, it can eventually be integrated into our conscious sense of self. However, if we try to ignore it, the shadow will make its presence felt in a variety of ways.

The Shadow Knows

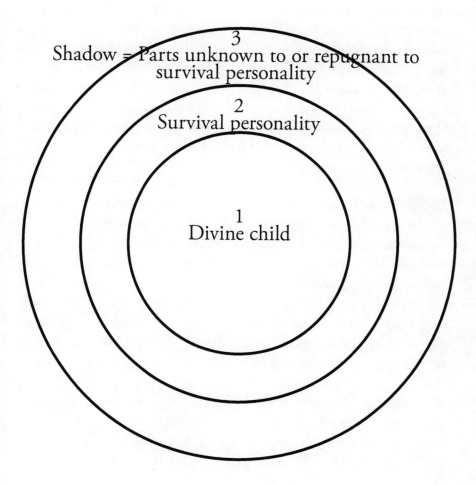

3
Shadow = Parts unknown to or repugnant to
survival personality

2
Survival personality

1
Divine child

Figure Fourteen

The first way that the shadow will let us know of its presence is through our "acting out" in certain ways that are not typical of our everyday behavior. Let us look at an example. Perhaps we have a controlled, uptight, anal-retentive sort of personality. Every move that we make is calculated and measured. Whatever we might think about this state of affairs, what then is to happen to our wild, spontaneous side? We keep that carefully under wraps to such an extent that we do not even know that we have this wild side. On the surface, everything seems to be going along smoothly, the spontaneous part of ourselves behind lock and key, but then this repressed part of us suddenly breaks loose. Let us say that we are at an office Christmas party, perhaps we have had a few drinks, and we find ourselves acting in a loud, playful, and even flirtatious way. Where did this person come from who is suddenly the life of the party? This is part of our shadow side, the part that we do our best to keep under wraps.

There is an old Latin expression, *"In vino, veritas"*, which means roughly, "With wine, the truth comes out." Alcohol or drugs serve to weaken the controls and let down the guard. It is often part of "acting out" for us humans. The substances not only facilitate the acting out process, they also provide a cover for it. The next day, for example, we can always blame our behavior on the drink. As the Irish expression says, "It was the creature." What these rationalizations fail to admit, however, is that the "creature" did not cause the behavior at all. It merely made it easier for the behavior to come out.

With the example of the office Christmas party, we might not worry too much. After all, it was only "letting off steam," and by the next morning, everything is back to normal and it is as if nothing ever happened. But what if the acting out causes disastrous consequences? This kind of thing can and does happen.

Two examples come to mind, both in the sexual arena. The fact that sexuality is part of our shadow side should not surprise us. We will be exploring some possible reasons for this suppression in our next chapter on "Anger and Sexuality". These particular examples both come from real life. There is no judgment implied of the individuals involved. Their situations are chosen because they provide a graphic depiction, I think, of the hell to pay when we ignore our shadow side.

The first example has to do with televangelist Jimmy Swaggart. No one was more convincing than Reverend Swaggart when he ranted and railed about the evils of sin, especially sexual sin. Most of us saw his convincing performances on television. Unbeknownst to us, however, was the fact that Reverend Swaggart, a married man, would regularly visit prostitutes in cheap motels, sometimes directly after speaking to us on television.

Again, I judge no one. I cast no stones. But this behavior is a graphic example of our shadow side bursting out just when we thought we had it under wraps. Perhaps surprisingly, I do not think that Reverend Swaggart's behavior could necessarily be written off as hypocrisy. He might have believed every word that he preached. But what he was incapable of doing was acknowledging the fact that the tendencies that he condemned in others were also amply present inside himself. In the shadows, perhaps, but present nonetheless.

The second example in the sexual arena that comes to mind would be pedophilia among Roman Catholic priests. In seminary formation, young men are told to be "other Christs". If this injunction is taken too literally, it can lead to an identification with the ideal self and a denial of one's shadow side, namely, that part of us that is and always will be far from being Christ-like. Throw into this mix the Catholic tendency for the laity to project their ideal side onto their clergy and you have a recipe for disaster.

One can argue about the statistics concerning sexual abuse among the Catholic clergy, but the bottom line is that every diocese in the country has been affected. There are thousands of victims who have come forward and hundreds of millions of dollars that have already been paid out in legal settlements. Any bishop in the country will tell you (in private) that this problem is one of the biggest ones facing the Church today.

What is this problem all about and why have so many Catholic priests been shown to be predators? First of all, when you are told that you are an *alter Christus* (another Christ) this can lead to what Jung called "inflation." One can become grandiose, buying into the image of oneself as being superhuman, greater than other earthly mortals. This is guaranteed to activate the shadow and drive it underground.

The other factor that comes into play here is that, when you think that you are greater than other human beings, you will not be interested in a relationship with equals. You will seek a relationship with those who will idolize you, and consider you to be greater than them. Who better to do this with than children who are younger, less educated, less powerful, more desirous of approval, and more prone to hero worship?

I do not wish to oversimplify this subject. I fully realize that there are many other factors that contribute to the creation of a pedophile or an ephebophile (attraction to adolescents). But a big part of the problem has to do with narcissistic infantile grandiosity, that then activates one's human side in its most instinctual expression. What more "fitting" way to unconsciously get in contact with this dimension than through sex with a child? This activity, while feeding into one's grandiosity, unconsciously has a way of bringing the individual back down to earth.

There is an interesting example of grandiosity being neutralized that is recounted in the Bible in the book of Daniel. King Nebuchadnezzar has lived for seven years with the belief that he is the equivalent of God. Daniel sees this when he interprets a dream for the king. What Daniel cannot foresee is the marvelous way in which the king's shadow side will assert itself. The king ends up spending the next seven years crawling on the ground and growling like an animal. An extreme within the psyche needed to be counterbalanced by its opposite extreme.

The king's dream points out that dreams are another way for the psyche to help us deal with our shadow. An example from my own life illustrates this fact. Back in 1977, I was undergoing the final stages of a spiritual metamorphosis that had been going on for two years. I was in a period of deep spiritual depression, convinced that I was worthless and hopeless. On the night when I hit rock bottom with this state of consciousness, I had the most glorious dream of my life. It was of a technicolor waterfall with a lovely sound that I can still hear to this day. When I awoke, I remember thinking to myself, "Anyone who has a dream that beautiful can't be all that bad."

Sometimes the dream will bring us down to earth, sometimes the dream will lift us out of a funk. This illustrates rather well, I think, that the shadow has little to do with good or evil. It has to do with balance and wholeness.

Shadow dreams are among the most common ones for people. Here we are speaking about the proverbial nightmares. Usually this consists of some sinister figure…Count Dracula, King Kong, Frankenstein, etc.…who is chasing us. We are running away from the figure for all that we are worth, our legs are getting heavier and heavier, and then-voila-we awake. Usually, we awaken in a state of anxiety, with our hearts pounding, sometimes in a cold sweat.

Who or what is that monster? It represents our shadow, some part of ourselves that we have labeled as monstrous. It is not actually bad in any real way. It is just that we have chosen to call it bad and monstrous because it does not fit into the image of ourselves that we try to project to the world.

Well, then, what does the monster want? It only wants to be accepted. Note that the monster does not destroy us. It is, instead, merely chasing us. This is stating, psychologically, that we are running away from some part of ourselves that wants to be accepted. If we can ever bring ourselves to accept every part of ourselves when we are conscious, when we are awake, then the nightmare will cease.

The word "nightmare" comes from the Latin word *mar* which means the sea. The sound "ma" is the same origin for Mary, mama, Madonna, etc. It symbolizes our psychic depths. All life comes from the oceans. We, too, as individuals, come from the amniotic fluid of our mother's wombs, our own saltwater home of origin. What is evil about any of that? Nothing. Nor is there anything evil about our nightmares. These dreams are simply here to tell us that we have split off parts of ourselves. These parts have taken up their abode in our unconscious. They seek to be integrated, to be blessed, to be welcomed as abandoned parts of ourselves. When we consciously welcome them back to us, usually after doing psychotherapy or some other type of deep work, the nightmares will disappear. Other monsters may again appear later. This just means that the psyche is waiting to embrace even more of our abandoned selves.

Accepting our shadow and blessing it and integrating it does not imply, for a second, that we should be "acting out." Nothing could be farther from the truth. But here is the paradox: when we do not face our shadow, we are *more likely* to "act out". Facing the shadow, acknowledging its existence, actually relieves some of the pressure that we feel inside us. To the extent that we run away from the shadow, to that extent it will pursue us. To the extent that we acknowledge it, to that extent it will be more manageable.

Shadow dreams frequently produce anxiety, or, rather, point out an underlying anxiety that already exists. They are usually not much fun. But an undealt-with shadow can produce something more troublesome: psychosomatic illnesses.

We have already dealt with psychosomatic illnesses extensively in Chapter Seven. Here let us just take note that when we are out of touch with some aspect of ourselves, our shadow side, the body will sometimes try to get our attention. It will do so by mimicking with the body what is happening on deeper levels. We already saw an example of that with King Nebuchadnezzar acting like an animal to bring him down to earth. People will, in analogous ways, often develop symptoms that will point out to them some aspect of themselves that needs to be integrated.

The Shadow in Mythology

Since we are all fragmented, and, to one degree or another, in denial about it, it stands to reason that our myths should deal with the theme of the shadow. Indeed they do, extensively. It is beyond the scope of this book to deal with the matter in depth. Here just let us just take a look at a few stories from mythology, old and new, that touch upon this vital subject.

One of the first that comes to mind is *Dr. Jekyll and Mr. Hyde*. When Robert Louis Stevenson wrote this book, he was asked where the idea for the book came from. He replied that it came from one of his dreams.

At the time this book was written, England was in its Victorian period. This was a time of propriety, social convention, and sexual repression. Only one side of one's self was honored: the controlled, civilized side. So what was one to do with this other side? Keep it under wraps. This was a classical situation where one's shadow side, in this case one's instinctual side, had to be kept below the surface.

We are probably all familiar with the theme of *Dr. Jekyll and Mr. Hyde*. Briefly, the protagonist works during the day as the altruistic Dr. Jekyll. As a servant of society, he is the epitome of living one's life at the service of others. In living such a life, however, what happens to one's own needs? They may go into the shadows of the unconscious. In this case, that shadow side manifests itself at night under the guise of the homicidal Mr. Hyde. (note the play-on-words of Hyde/hide) This side of the personality murders prostitutes. Then, as the sun comes up again, Mr. Hyde rushes home and reverts to the revered Dr. Jekyll.

Killing the prostitutes is a vain attempt to kill off the instinctual, unbridled free part of himself. Needless to say, this never works and Mr. Hyde is no exception. The protagonist ends badly, as is always the case when people are living such a fractured life.

Another variation of this theme of the shadow is the story of *Beauty and the Beast*. In essence, this centuries-old tale is about a figure that is hated and feared because he is judged to be ugly. He is not a bad individual in any way. He is just considered to be repulsive according to the standards of his society. The Beast lives by himself in a house on a hill. In a similar way, we isolate the parts of ourselves that we consider to be ugly, to be repulsive to others, and this isolation cuts off an essential part of our primal self.

No one will have anything to do with the Beast until Beauty comes along. After overcoming her own resistances, Beauty accepts the Beast as he is. Who could ever forget the scene in Disney's rendition of the classic when Beauty and the Beast dance together? With his cravat neatly in place, Beast is light on his feet, pirouetting around the room gracefully and freely. This is a perfect dramatization of how, when we embrace our shadow, it ceases to be experienced as ugly but is, instead, miraculously transformed into a thing of grace that helps us to dance our way through life.

By the way, notice that Disney Productions is making a conscious effort to bring these mythological themes to the big screen. The above-mentioned films, along with _The Hunchback of Notre Dame_, _The Little Mermaid_, _The Lion King_ and others, are proof positive of the enduring power of archetypal stories, particularly those dealing with acceptance of various parts of ourselves.

No mention of the shadow in mythology would be complete without talking about _The Phantom of the Opera_. This modern day myth, transformed into a theatrical production, is a wonderful story about acceptance of one's shadow.

The phantom is, once again, a physically hideous creature. There is nothing evil about him at all. In fact, he has much to offer Christine. He will help her with her creativity, he will help her in her relationship, but first he demands something. He wants to be accepted. Initially, Christine, like all of the others, rejects him. This is not a smart move.

For, although the phantom is not a bad creature, he can be troublesome when he is ignored.

Initially spurned, the phantom retreats to where he dwells: in the bowels of The Opera House of Paris. This reminds me of a quote from Jung: "The gods have become diseases. Zeus no longer rules Olympus but rather the solar plexus and produces curious specimens for the doctor's consulting room or disorders in the brains of politicians and journalists who unwittingly let loose psychic epidemics on the world."[9] What this quote is getting at is that the rejected parts of ourselves (in this case the gods and goddesses who are personifications of psychological principles), end up causing somatic symptoms. Often these are gastrointestinal problems like ulcers, colitis, constipation, irritable bowel syndrome, etc. The shadow will be heard, or our bodies will pay the price.

At the end of the play, Christine does accept the phantom. In fact, she dramatically shows this by kissing him on the lips. When she does this, everything changes, everything shifts. Now the phantom does not want anything from her; in fact, he willingly relinquishes her to the young man who would be the perfect partner for her.

What did Christine do to merit this change of heart and change of behavior? She embraced her shadow. It was the spiritual part of her that did this. Note that her name is Christine, clearly a Christ figure, clearly a symbol of the true self. The same thing happens to us when we can embrace the discarded parts of ourselves that live in the shadows. It is a classical win/win situation. The discarded parts are happy because they have been recognized, and we are enriched because we have more qualities and energies that are now available to us. All it takes is a generous hug, a generous embrace on our part of the rejected parts of ourselves.

Years ago, I shared these hard-won insights with a young woman who was embarking upon religious life to become a nun. She was having terrible nightmares that were very distressful. When we spoke a bit about her situation, it became clear what the problem was. In trying to identify with her ideal self, she was not accepting her shadow. Once this was done (and it is never an easy thing to do), her nightmares stopped. She wrote a poem about her situation. This is her poem, simple yet very profound, which shall remain anonymous.

Hug Your Shadow

What's this? An ominous shadow
Which rears its frightening head,
And follows me around my day
Then waits beside my bed.

I don't know where it's come from,
Or what its purpose be.
I only know it haunts my life
And makes me feel "un free".

I've got to face this shadow
And find out what it is.
I can't ignore its presence,
It's there, it stalks, it lives!

Now tell me why you bother
And follow me around?
You're making life a nightmare
And running me aground.

But when I faced that shadow
I was aghast to see
That what I feared to come to know
Was really only ME!

That shadow, like a child,
Rejected and disliked
Was only saying, "I am YOU,
Accept me, it's all right!"

Now shadow doesn't frighten me
Nor at my conscious tug.
I looked, I saw, I gave to it
A great big friendly hug.

It was tough for my client to embrace her shadow. It entailed a kind of ego reduction. But, in the end, she was blessed because of her ability to do this courageous inner work. Jung points out that, not only is the individual blessed, but the society benefits as well. He reasoned that the projection of the shadow onto others represents the greatest danger of our time.

The classical example of this shadow projection happened during World War II. Adolf Hitler had sold to the German people the notion that they were the master race. They were Aryans, pure blooded, noble and gifted. The German people, for various reasons, were only too willing to believe this. There was only one problem with this line of thinking: what to do with the individual and collective shadow of the German people. What happened, initially, was that their shadow went underground, into their unconscious. It was only a matter of time before this unconsciously repressed shadow began to be projected outwards. All that was undesirable was projected onto the Jews, the Slavs, the gypsies, the handicapped, and the homosexuals. The unconscious thinking was that, in eliminating all of these "undesirables," they would be able to eliminate the pressure from within themselves. The pressure was coming from the group soul which was seeking balance. It was as if the soul was saying, "You are not all pure. You are, like everyone, a mixture of all things." The Germans simply could not stand this dose of reality. We all know what happened as a result of their inability to do so.

It should be emphasized here that the German people were not some monsters. Creating them in that image was a function of the projection of our own national shadow. The fact of the matter is that, historically, the German people were highly cultured, educated, religious, even mystical. Perhaps it was because their past achievements were so great that they were "set up" for this projection of their national shadow.

Wholesale projection also goes on between the races. Reggie White, a Hall of Fame bound African-American football player, said that "most whites are good at making money". I can introduce him to thousands of whites who do not qualify. And, of course, so many white people still look on African Americans as lazy, lawbreaking, sex machines. The fact that all data show the vast majority of African Americans as just the opposite is apparently beside the point. Sometimes the projections are based on something having to do with reality; sometimes the projection is constructed from whole cloth. The point is that it is unfair and unhelpful to project our own shadow onto others. For when we project elements of ourselves onto others, we fragment ourselves, unfairly make others carry our shadow, and endanger the fragile web of life.

One of the ironies of shadow work is that awareness of one's shadow often indicates spiritual growth. Look at it this way. On a cloudy day, we do not see any shadows cast in nature. But, let a little sunlight begin to peek through, and we begin to see the play of shadows around us. Let the sun shine brightly and the shadows are sharp and precisely defined. Spiritually, it works the same way. When we are walking around in the fog, we are unaware of our repressed shadow that has perhaps been projected onto others. Let a bit of spiritual illumination come into our life, however, and we begin to be aware of our shadow. If a real spiritual awakening should happen, we see our repressed shadow material loud and clear.

Mythology backs up this insight. The hero is often portrayed as being on a mythic quest to find the Holy Grail. Literally, the grail represents the chalice used by Jesus at the Last Supper. That was the theme of the Indiana Jones movie, _The Last Crusade_. The Holy Grail, however, is actually about a lot more than finding a chalice. Symbolically it has always stood for the true self. Finding the Holy Grail is the same as finding who we really are. These grail legends speak of the hero going deep into the dark woods (i.e. the unconscious). Along the way, he or she must do battle with various demons and dragons. The biggest and the worst of the dragons, however, does not appear at the beginning of the journey. This dragon is a guardian at the threshold of the Holy Grail. In other words, your toughest trial will be right before you find what you are looking for.

The same thing happens on our own inner quest. The shadow is found deep within us. It is a sign that we are actually close to our true self when the spectre of the shadow appears. It is when we are most afraid of what we see within ourselves that we are on the brink of our greatest breakthrough. In the West, we speak of slaying one's dragon. In the East, people speak about outwitting the dragon by sneaking around it. Whatever metaphor is used, the bottom line is that spiritual growth entails dealing with and owning and coming to terms with the part of ourselves that does not fit.

It should be emphasized again that the shadow is not evil. It just represents the part that does not fit with the ideal image we have of ourselves. Since most of us are consciously trying to be decent people, our shadow will frequently take on the guise of some sinister figure. It is that aspect of ourselves that scares us. But a person who is consciously a criminal may find themselves being pursued in their dreams by Mother Theresa or Saint Francis of Assisi. It is the possibility of that aspect of themselves being present that causes the criminal to break into a cold sweat!

The Shadow and Evil

Lest there be some confusion on the matter, it is important to make a distinction here between the shadow and radical evil. As I have tried to do throughout the book, I will try to avoid theological and metaphysical discussions. Instead, let us stay with psychological descriptions that help us distinguish one from the other.

The shadow represents parts of our primal self that have been split off. As such, these parts are fundamentally good. They have something to offer us. They may not fit the ideal image that we have of ourselves, they may humiliate us and embarrass us, but they are part of us, part of the being of the divine child.

When we encounter our shadow, we may be afraid. But our shadow does not want to hurt us. It only wants to be accepted and be a part of the team again. Even in our nightmare dreams, notice that the monster pursuing us does not hurt us. In fact, it never even lays a hand on us. It can't. That is the point. We are running away from some part of ourselves that we have made into a monster, and all it wants is to be accepted. When you think of the shadow, think as an example of the Lion, the Scarecrow and the Tin Man from _The Wizard of Oz_. They are fearful and not too smart and rigid, but they are not bad characters. They all want to help Dorothy on the journey.

Radical evil, on the other hand, wants to obliterate our very existence. It is a voice within all of us that wants to discount our worth, our intrinsic value. It is a voice that tells us to kill ourselves and tries to ruin the good that we are accomplishing. This voice wants us to disappear, to be crushed.

All spiritual traditions, whatever their theological explanations, tell us to stand up to this voice and fight it. These traditions are steering us in the right directions. We would be foolish to listen to the voice of self destruction. It is not our ally but our enemy.

174

When you think of radical evil, think of the character of the Wicked Witch from the West in _The Wizard of Oz_. This force in the psyche does not like to see us grow. That is why the Wicked Witch did everything she could to derail Dorothy from her spiritual journey. Of course, when Dorothy stood up to the Wicked Witch and threw a bucket of water on her, the Witch melted down before our very eyes. In similar ways, when we can stand up to the life-denying voice within us, it too will melt down and lose its power to hurt us.

I want to be clear here: We are to hug our shadow but we are to stand up to the voices of destruction. They are two different voices entirely with two different agendas.

The Unlived Life

One final aspect of the shadow has to do with what is called the unlived life. For various reasons, usually having to do with how we have been indoctrinated, aspects of our lives have been banished to our unconscious, never, we hope, to see the light of day. Such banishment may appear to work for a while, but there is inevitably a day of reckoning. As an old commercial used to say, "It isn't nice to fool Mother Nature."

Let's take an example of this excision of a part of who we are with its banishment to the unconscious. Perhaps when we were younger we were taught to always keep our nose to the grindstone, to never waste a minute, to work hard at all times. Obviously, there is nothing wrong with being industrious. But, in the process of working so hard, whatever happened to fun, to spontaneity, to being playful, to deep relaxation? It was all put on hold, perhaps with the thought that, at least in this lifetime, we would never get to experience any of it.

All those repressed tendencies never really go away; they just go underground. In such instances, what may happen is that these needs may assert themselves later on in life. We may experience the emergence of all of these areas in our life when the timing is right. The emergence may frighten us at first, because these tendencies may not fit into the image of ourselves that we have carefully constructed. But, if we can relax and find ways to allow these repressed parts to join our sense of self again, we will be infinitely richer for the experience.

Please notice that growing spiritually does not imply a running away from reality. It entails, instead, facing every part of ourselves and of the world, the good, the bad, and the ugly. Those who hold up a disembodied ideal of spiritual growth have completely missed the point. We are challenged to become, not ethereal and transcendent, but fully human and fully alive.

Nowhere is this truth more apparent than in the tendency of some religious teachings that would have us run away from our instincts, especially sexuality and anger. Our next chapter will demonstrate how sexuality and anger are not just compatible with spiritual growth, but are actually part of the spiritual journey itself.

CHAPTER THIRTEEN

Anger and Sexuality: Allies on the Journey

While the shadow represents the past that does not fit into the ego ideal of many people, one could say virtually the same thing about anger and sexuality. Many religious searchers have been led to believe that anger and sexuality have no place on a spiritual path. This chapter will try to set the record straight, and show that anger and sexuality are an integral part of the journey to wholeness.

As I sit down to write this chapter, it occurs to me that I have unconsciously put off writing it until the end of the book. This is typical behavior for many spiritual types who are just not sure where to put anger and sexuality in their lives.

Traditionally, spirituality seems to imply for many people a flight to things otherworldly. It elicits images of light, transcendence, higher vibrations and blissful states of consciousness. While those elements are meant to be part of the journey (although many religious types report having very little experience of any of it), authentic spirituality is meant to be inclusive of our earthly dimensions as well.

I think it is fair to say that many religious or spiritual traditions have never gotten this point. Religious organizations tend to ignore dealing with the visceral dimensions of the human body.

Since so many people tend to compartmentalize spirituality into the realm of the other-worldly, they often do not know what to do with anger and sexuality, which are so rooted in the body. For example, flip through the program offerings by the major consciousness centers around the country. There is lots to say about how to get out of the body, and very little to say about how to deal with the so-called "lower" experiences of anger and sexuality. Yet I am personally convinced that any authentic spirituality worth its salt will find a way to integrate anger and sexuality as *part of* the spiritual journey.

What They Have In Common

If we are willing to concede that anger and sexuality need to be integrated into our spiritual path, the next question has to do with why we are talking about them in the same chapter. What do they have in common? Don't they deal with two entirely different emotions?

Anger and sexuality have often been spoken of in the same breath because, when we are in their throes, we feel out of control. And, if there is one thing that frightens most people, it is being out of control.

Take anger, for instance. When we are caught up in its full force, we feel flushed. Our heart is pounding. Our hands shake. Our voices quiver and raise an octave. Perhaps, in the past, we have slammed doors, kicked things, broken dishes, slapped or punched someone. We may have said hideous things that have permanently damaged relationships. Our anger may have caused us to walk out of a job without having thought through all of the implications. Anger is dangerous! It can be dangerous to our health, to our property, to our loved ones, and to our livelihood. No wonder so many people are afraid of it.

And look at the trouble we can get into with sex. Every day we read about people who rape or molest or even kill for sex. We hear about unwanted pregnancies. We are reminded about the repercussions of unsafe sex. There is AIDS and other sexually transmitted diseases, some of which are fatal. Sexual drives can destroy marriages, derail people from their careers, even end up leading people behind bars. No wonder people are afraid of sex! So much can go wrong when we get involved with it. Is it any wonder that people are so wary of the power of sex?

Anger, Sex, and Spirituality

On face value, they seem to have very little in common. Anger and sex "lower" our consciousness; spirituality raises it. Anger and sex appear to have much in common with our animal nature; spirituality seems to refer to the angelic, even divine side of our nature. This sort of thinking, so typical of the way most people view the subject, is actually close to the truth. But the operative word here is "close." The notion that anger and sex are enemies of spirituality is a classical example of a partial truth.

In themselves, anger and sexuality are not the enemies of anything. When they are regulated, coordinated, and put at the service of the self, they not only enrich our lives, but even help us tune into our spiritual nature. However, when unregulated and uncoordinated and allowed to romp around at will, they can make our lives a living hell.

The key, then, seems to be that we need to be in charge of these drives and not the other way around. That cannot happen through denial and repression and shame. What we need to do is to find the Self at the core of our being, this "still point of the turning world" (T. S. Eliot).[10] This part of us can then orchestrate every part of our being, calling upon it when necessary, and telling it to be quiet when that is the right thing to do.

The Self functions precisely like the conductor of a symphony orchestra. A good conductor lets each musician play when it is their turn, yet the conductor is clearly in charge. The conductor knows how to silence a musician when that is appropriate. All is done at the service of the masterpiece. Everyone gets to play their part, yet only according to a master plan. If each musician plays whenever they want to, we do not have a symphony orchestra; we have cacophony. In the same way, anger and sex have their role in the symphony of our lives. But, even though these energies tend to be "prima donnas," they cannot be allowed to run away with things. The Self must always be in charge.

However, there is a Catch-22 in the above scenario, a real paradox. And it is this: in order to *discover* the Self, we have to find a way to quiet down the impulses of anger and sex. Later in life, anger and sex can be trusted to support the symphony of our lives. In the early days, however, anger and sex have to be disciplined.

The word "discipline," I realize, is an unwelcome word to many people. That is because it has often been associated with repression. However, the word actually comes from the Latin word that means "student". So the idea here is that we have to become students and learn some impulse control. Children cannot be allowed to "act out' however they want to when it comes to anger and sex. The formation in this regard need have nothing to do with shame and guilt. It can all be framed positively, inviting the child to master their impulses for the purpose of having a more fulfilling life.

There are two pitfalls to avoid: 1) implying that there is something shameful about the impulse in question; and 2) insinuating that we should repress the impulse rather than find a way to coordinate it with our total life.

Shaming

When we try to make people feel badly about their God-given natural impulses, we do them a terrible disservice. We set people on a war-like footing against themselves. We virtually guarantee that they will end up with chronic, low-grade depression, and we flirt with the possibility of pushing them into a splitting of the psyche.

The simple truth of the matter is that anger and sex are drives that are innate to the human species. To use a computer analogy, they are a part of our hard wiring. They are not software. Anger and sex are common to every one of us. To imply that there is something innately wrong with these impulses is to start the person on the road to self-hatred. Alienation and sickness are bound to ensue. How can they not?

An example comes to mind. Let us call him John. Handsome, virile, charismatic, with a very strong sex drive. There was only one thing wrong. He was ashamed of his sex drive. He had been brought up in a sexually repressed family where sex was considered "barnyard activity." God permitted it for the continuation of the human race, but it was not something to be enjoyed. John's quandary was that he enjoyed sex very much. In fact, he had what we would call a hyperactive sex drive. He wanted sex with his wife more than once a day. This was beginning to put a strain on the marriage, since the drive was so obsessional in nature. However, that was not the real problem. The real problem was that he felt intensely guilty about having sex at all. The lights had to be out. He would never look at his wife when having sex. Worst of all, he would refuse to discuss any aspect of the their sex life. It was all cloaked in shame, a taboo subject.

John, who happened to be a fundamentalist Christian, handled sex like many religious types do: he compartmentalized it. It had nothing to do with love, nothing to do with creativity, and certainly nothing to do with spirituality. It was this animal drive that God permitted for a specific purpose, but it was not something of which to be proud. It was not something to bless and integrate and celebrate. It was a drive to be appeased that had nothing to do with the whole of his life.

Let us now look at an example of shaming concerning the expression of anger. For this, I need look no further than my own family of origin. I grew up in a family where anger was not expressed or tolerated. I checked this out with my two brothers and my sister, and none of us can even remember a single example of my mother or father fighting or disagreeing about anything, let alone getting angry in front of us. This was done for a good and calculated reason: they wished to raise their children in a happy home. We now find out that they used to have

181

their arguments in the bedroom, behind closed doors. However, we children never saw any of it. The unintended side effect of all this was to communicate the fact that there is something wrong with anger. For, as children, we would certainly get angry. Someone would take our toy or would offend us in one of a thousand ways. But, whenever we would feel offended and show any anger at all, we would be sent upstairs to our room. I can still remember hearing, "If you are going to act that way, go upstairs to your room." This felt like a banishment, a shaming. At the very least, I "got" the message that there was something wrong with anger.

The shaming around anger and sex was reinforced by my Catholic school conditioning. Again, let us be clear that the goal was a good one: learn not to be controlled by anger and sex. Those who do not learn this lesson often end up in prison or dead. What was overdone was the means to fostering this control: making children feel that there is something wrong with them if they ever felt angry or sexual.

Ideal images were held up to us to emulate. They were most often the saints. It always came across that the saints were better than us. One of the reasons that this was so had to do with the fact that the saints did not get angry. Nor were they sexual. Saints never complained. They suffered every indignity as a way of suffering along with Jesus on the cross. Plus the saints were almost all celibate. Or people who were married and then became celibate after their spouses died.

It is all so laughable now. Of course, saints got angry! And there are millions of undeclared saints who enjoyed a lusty sex life. It is just that those saints were virtually never declared to be saints by the Catholic Church.

Think of what the above type of conditioning did to young, impressionable minds. It made us landing strips for every neurosis imaginable. Of course, not every youngster was formed in this manner. It is characteristic primarily of Catholics who grew up in the 50's and 60's. But Christians of every kind may be able to relate to certain aspects of it. And, perhaps somewhat surprisingly, many Jewish people report that there were similar aspects of dysfunctionality in their formation.

The repressive, alienating teachings about sexuality even had us feeling guilty about our thoughts. Psychologists today tell us that males typically have sexual thoughts hundreds of times per day. This is just the way the Creator made us. However, imagine what sort of internal warfare is set up when a healthy adolescent boy feels that he is immoral hundreds of times a day because of his "dirty" thoughts. I can remember the confession line at the church attached to the high school I attended. There were always boys (and a few girls) lined up to unburden themselves to the priest about their "dirty" thoughts and "impure" touching of themselves and others.

When I saw the movie Pleasantville I remember thinking to myself that I knew the town very well. I grew up there. It was truly an age of innocence. All adults could be trusted. Everybody got along. And everyone controlled their sexual expression to such an extent that sexuality was buried deep within the body and within the psyche.

My brother John and I discussed the movie recently. We both enjoyed it, but he wondered why most of the awakening focused on opening up sexually. I reminded him that this was the logical sequence of our awakening. Before there was the anger of protest against the Vietnam war, first there was Elvis Presley. And James Dean. And Jerry Lee Lewis. Only later did the anger come. We began to feel alive when we began to feel sexual.

One of the rules in dysfunctional homes is not to feel anything. That is because feelings are "dangerous." I can still remember being taught in the seminary to be wary of feelings. Is there some truth here? Of course; it just has to do with degree. Because *some* feelings can *sometimes* get us into trouble, does this mean that we should shut down all of our feelings? Obviously not. Yet this is close to what happened in Christianity, especially in Catholicism. The result? It all went underground, to surface later in Crusades and pogroms and ethnic cleansing, all in the name of God. It also found expression in sadistic acts like the torture of the Inquisition and the masochism of self-flagellation.

There were times in the history of Christianity when anger was effectively sublimated. Great movements of social justice like the creation of labor unions would be an example. So would the role that the Catholic Church played in the dismantling of the Soviet empire. However, in studying the history of the Christian churches, I have yet to see a time when it got things completely right when it comes to sex. I am always telling people that they do not need to go to the East in order to find a vibrant spirituality. When it comes to sex, however, that is the one exception to the rule. The churches have never quite known how to get this one right.

Judaism has done a much better job of it than Christianity in this regard. For example, in certain expressions of Judaism, people are *expected* to have sexual relations with their spouse on the Sabbath. Since it is a holy thing to do, why not do it on a holy day? In Christianity, on the other hand, the attitude is more like, "Never on Sunday." There is a certain internal logic to this way of bizarre thinking. If it is seen as dirty, a kind of barnyard activity at best, then one should avoid doing it on a holy day. In fact, in certain circles of Catholicism, *abstaining from* sex was advocated as a way of preparing oneself to receive the sacraments.

Reframing Anger and Sexuality

What is needed here, I think, is a paradigm shift. We need to unlearn so much of what we have been taught. We need to see our humanity as fundamentally good, not something from which to escape. Anger and sexuality need to be restored to their rightful place in our lives. They are not only not an impediment, they are essential allies on the journey to spiritual wholeness. (See Figure 15)

Anger and Sexuality

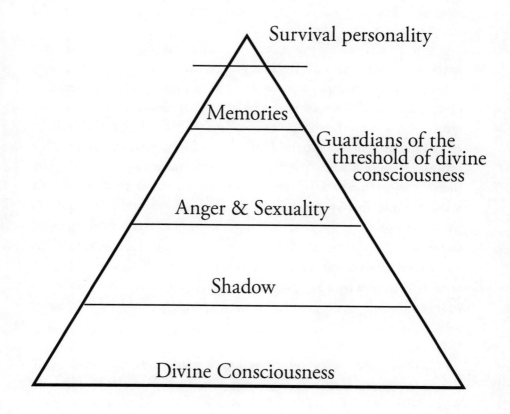

Survival personality

Memories

Guardians of the
threshold of divine
consciousness

Anger & Sexuality

Shadow

Divine Consciousness

Figure Fifteen

Of course, when humanity has been so wary about these aspects of human life for so long, there is probably something to be wary about. Sheer license is not the answer. Upholding the right of all Americans to keep and bear arms may be the unstated goal of the NRA, but it hardly seems on the cutting edge of human evolution. Nor are group orgies or the sexual exploitation of children. Religious conservatives need to have their voices heard. They are warning us about the need for self control as individuals and as a society. Yet their brand of shaming and repression hardly seems like the solution either.

The key to this dilemma is an old-fashioned word with modern applications: sublimation. The sublimation that I am advocating implies getting to know anger and sexuality and then lifting it, consecrating it to a higher level. The old brand of sublimation that many of us were taught skipped the first step of accepting one's feelings and drives. It sort of did an end run around it all. In so doing, it short-circuited the process. This resulted in passive/aggressive behavior in religious circles that is truly problematic. Since people were not encouraged to feel their anger because they were ashamed of their feelings, the anger initially went underground. Of course, it never truly goes away. The repressed anger eventually comes out in behavior like forgetting, showing up late, and other indirect expressions of anger. The undealt-with sexuality comes out in pornography, pedophilia, chronic masturbation, and other indirect ways of dealing with the need to have a healthy adult sexual relationship.

No, skipping the step of getting to know ourselves is no answer at all. We need to experience our anger and our sexuality, make friends with these essential components of human life, and then learn how to use them to serve us and serve the world. An analogy might be helpful here. It is the analogy of training wild horses. When a wild horse is first captured and corralled, it is mean and dangerous. In fact, wild horses have been known to stomp to death people who get too close to them. The horse trainer needs to go very slowly at first. Riding the horse at this point is out of the question. The process begins, instead, with the trainer standing outside the pen, letting him or herself be seen and smelled by the horse. The trainer talks to the horse. Eventually, the trainer ventures the lightest of touches through the slats in the fence. Then maybe the briefest attempt at petting the horse. When the horse is used to that, the trainer climbs in the corral. Then comes the muzzling. Then the saddling, all with the utmost of care and patience. Finally, after all of those steps are taken, the trainer is ready to mount the horse. If all goes as planned, it is a classical win/win situation. The horse gets to ride the open range again, and the owner of the horse gets to ride it. If the horse is kept penned up indefinitely, however, its spirit will be broken and it will just get meaner and be good for nothing.

In the same way, our anger and sexuality need to be explored in small ways at first. As a two year old, for example, if we cry and protest because we do not want to do something, those around us should not try to shame us. We are allowed to say no. This is actually good training in setting proper boundaries for ourselves. When we are teenagers, it is perfectly natural to be rebellious. The angry young man or woman is a necessary stage in our growth. We need to be able to enter fully into this experience. If we shut it down prematurely, we will never experience what the raw emotion of anger feels like. Therapist's offices are crowded with people who skipped over these steps. These are folks who never learned how to say no, who never learned how to maintain proper boundaries in life, who never learned how to stand up for themselves.

Sexuality, too, is something that we become comfortable with in incremental stages. When babies and little children touch their genitals, this is a natural process of discovery. When boys and girls develop crushes on one another, this is a healthy development. We should not then try to shame them. Later, they will attend parties where there will be kissing games. Again, perfectly natural. There will be dances and hayrides. Boys will have erections and wet dreams. Girls will have their periods and experience the growth of their breasts.

When all of this development is blessed, the individual will become comfortable with, at home with, his or her body. As a therapist, trust me, this does not always happen. Youngsters become arrested in their development all of the time. We have to spend lots of time helping individuals get in touch with their anger and their sexuality. For many people it has been a case of incomplete development at best.

Expressing Ourselves Fully

Once we know what anger and sexuality feel like, we can be the master of their expression. Anger can be used in a noble way to feel the outrage of social injustice. The goal in life is not to strive for a flatline brain reading. There is nothing wrong with passion and with compassion. We are allowed to care deeply and to invest ourselves seriously in the affairs of the world. In fact, it is only the *puer*, the little boy or girl, who never really grows up enough to truly care about this world.

The trick, however, is to be the master of our emotions. One of the early ways that this is done is by transcending narcissistic infantile grandiosity. When we do not expect everything and everybody in life to cater to our needs, we will not set up a lot of expectations, and we will not be so often disappointed. Buddha went so far as to say that expectation is the source of all suffering. We can learn to let go of and to lower our self-centered expectations in life. This is a way of cutting off anger at the pass. Living in the moment with what is, rather than what we want to be there, is a time-tested technique for spiritual growth.

Curbing such pretty outbursts of pique is a good start. However, we can also learn how to be angry in a way that serves the world. The first trick here is to approach things with a large perspective and not to take things personally. It is not about us. It is about what is right and what is wrong.

Three examples immediately come to mind: Rosa Parks, Gandhi, and Martin Luther King. Earlier, we looked at what these individuals did. Here we'll look at how they did it. The anger that they felt was never personalized. They refused to get "hooked' into being personally affronted by what was done to them. It was always about something larger than themselves.

There is a marvelous story about a Samurai warrior that is applicable here. The Samurai defended the borders and protected the weak and the children. That has always been the role of the spiritual warrior. One day the Samurai was told by the king to confront someone who was invading the realm. Note that the Samurai did not undertake this on his own. That is because the warrior within us must always be under the direction of the Self (the king/queen within). The Samurai confronted the enemy and raised his sword. Just when he was about to strike, the enemy spit in his face. Immediately, the Samurai put his sword back in his sheath without striking the man and walked away. Why? Because to strike at this time would have made it a personal act of retribution. The anger must be channeled and used, not to get even for a personal offense, but to serve a transpersonal goal. Rosa Parks, Gandhi, and Martin Luther King had mastered this lesson. They show us what a valuable thing anger can be when it is used in the right way.

When it comes to using sexuality for a higher purpose, we must turn, alas, to the East. For Eastern spirituality has found some marvelous ways of integrating sexuality as a way of tuning into our spiritual core. Specifically, I am referring to various forms of Tantra. In one form of this discipline, one learns to postpone orgasm and instead focus on the union of mind and heart that is mediated by the union of the body. Once again, it is not a personal thing. It is not about a conquest by the ego or the release of built up sexual tension. It is all about, to put it in religious terms, the union with God.

This does not mean that sexual love-making has to be overly serious. On the contrary, it can be spontaneous and playful and fun. However, the context of this form of love-making is transpersonal in nature. It is seen as an activity of the soul, channeled, directed to the higher goal of union with the Source.

Perhaps a good image for this kind of love-making is meditation. When the body is seen as a temple and the man and woman see themselves as a priest and a priestess, we are talking about sex as a spiritual discipline, a form of meditation. To the extent that we find this image difficult to deal with, to that extent we have alienated ourselves from the sacredness of the body. It is time for spiritual journeyers to reclaim every aspect of themselves, including sex, as a way of returning to their center.

The goal of the spiritual path is human wholeness. A byproduct of this wholeness is a transformation in consciousness. If we have been able to bless and integrate every aspect of ourselves, we will relate to life in a way no longer dominated by fear. We will begin to live our lives according to our full psychological and spiritual potential. Our next and final chapter will describe, in simple terminology, what spiritual consciousness looks and feels like.

CHAPTER FOURTEEN

Higher Ground

In the very beginning of this book, I underscored the point that there is no contradiction between psychological and spiritual health. In fact, to me they represent different disciplines that deal with the same reality: human consciousness and behavior. Psychology tends to deal with one end of the continuum (one's past and present problems), while spirituality tends to deal with one's full potential. (See Figure 16)

Psychology   Spirituality

$$\longleftarrow \hspace{6cm} \longrightarrow$$

Human Consciousness
(Fig. 16)

Certainly there is always some overlap. Psychology and spirituality represent different areas of the one continuum, but they both deal with human consciousness. Psychology could expand its interests to focus on what brings about joy, peace, love, creativity, and a sense of unity with all things. Spirituality, on the other hand, could show more interest in family of origin issues, which could color our growth in consciousness one way or the other. These shifts could happen, but, currently, psychology and spirituality do not seem to realize that they are different paths climbing up the same mountain.

As I mentioned earlier, only transpersonal psychology (and spiritual psychology) acknowledge the need to deal with one's full expansion of human consciousness as well as deal with one's past and present problems. However, let us deal in this chapter with what a fully expanded sense of consciousness looks like.

Sometimes the ultimate truth is expressed in terms of height and sometimes it is expressed in terms of depth. What these metaphors have in common is that there is universal consensus that the ultimate answer is not found in everyday, fear-based thinking.

The tendency, however, has often been to look outside ourselves for the answers. For thousands of years, people have thought that the answers to their quest for inner peace must lie in a teaching, or a spiritual master, in a philosophy of life, or in a religion. While all of these things may be helpful for some people, for others they actually may become an obstacle. This happens when the individual gives away his or her innate power, projecting it onto a religious leader, thus feeling weak, sinful, and unworthy.

Why people do this is a complicated matter, one that could be taken up in another book. But here the simple point is that Jesus, the Buddha, and mystics of every stripe from every religion have agreed that what we are looking for is found within us. Jesus put it this way, " The Kingdom of God is within you." (Luke 17:20-2 From <u>Good News Bible</u>, New York, American Bible Society, 1976) Despite all of this consistent teaching, 99% of the people on the planet still do not get it. Historically, they have never believed it; apparently they still do not believe it. Perhaps the message is too good to believe. Perhaps our shame is so great that we cannot possibly believe that there is anything divine within our broken clay pots, our earthen vessels that we call the human body.

A number of years ago, I attended a workshop given by a marvelous teacher by the name of Sebastian Temple. In that workshop, he gave us the words of a song based on an old Hindu story that is thousands of years old. I have changed the language to make it more inclusive, but here is this wonderful story that says it all.

"Where shall we hide the spirit from humans?"
The gods all cried when they were made
"How can we guard our secret now"
They asked each other so afraid.

Hide it in the earth and they will mine it
Hide it on a mountain and they will climb it
Even in the sea and they will find it
Where shall we hide the spirit from humans?

Quite beside themselves they cried
These upstarts will take our throne
We have made them far too smart
Not to claim our heaven as their home.

They thought of stars in outer space
Or in the nature of a tree.
But they knew that humans could solve
Each and every mystery.

Hide it in matter, they'll analyze it.
Hide it in water, they'll crystallize it.
Even in hell, they'll surmise it.
Where shall we hide the spirit from humans?

Then they solved the mystery
Of how the frightened gods should win.
The wisest said, Let's take the spirit
And hide it deep inside of them.

Hide it in their hearts and they will doubt it
Hide it in their minds and they will live without it
Even if we reveal and shout it
They will never believe – that the spirit is deep inside of them.

As we arrive at the conclusion of our tale, we are approaching what is called the ineffable. This means that our words and even our images come up short. The height of mysticism frequently ends with silence. There is much more to say, but words are inadequate. Sometimes symbols come to our rescue. Symbols are the language of the unconscious. However, often, even symbols do not adequately describe what we feel. For example, a circle says a lot and it says nothing. Meister Eckhart said that God is a circle whose center is everywhere, but whose circumference is nowhere. This is beautiful, but what does it communicate to a person who has never taken the spiritual path seriously?

It seems to me, then, that, with all due respect to words and symbols, they often conceal as much as they reveal. The only thing that is the real coin of the realm – spiritually – is *experience*. We cannot deny what we have experienced, and experience validates itself. It does not need any further explanation.

That having been said, let us take a look at what spiritual journeyers tell us has been the fruit of their journey. They all report basically the same thing. For what it is worth, this is what my experience has looked like as well. Because these experiences represent a treasure buried in a field, something that we are all desperately looking for, let us take a look at what this journey should hopefully result in for us. (See Figure 17)

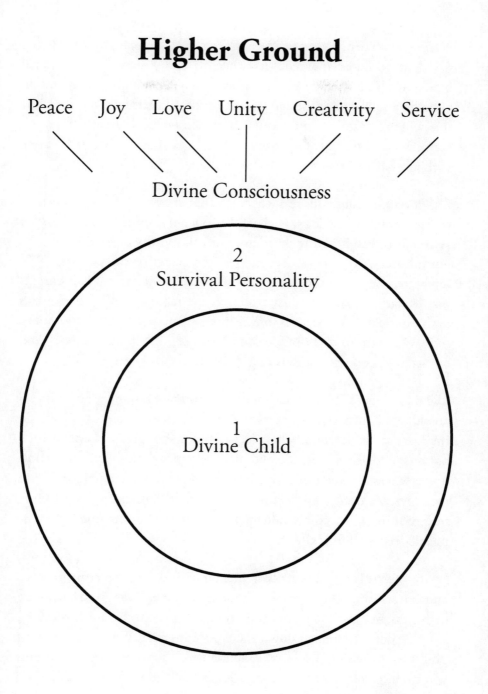

Higher Ground

Peace   Joy   Love   Unity   Creativity   Service

Divine Consciousness

2
Survival Personality

1
Divine Child

Figure Seventeen

1) Unity – When you read the writings of the great mystics of the world, it becomes apparent that they all had a sense of the radical interconnection of things. They spoke about all thoughts of separation as being an illusion of the ego (viz. the survival personality). They had this sense of cosmic consciousness in which one feels a part of nature, connected to all creatures, at one with all that has ever existed, at one with all that will ever be.

Call it cosmic consciousness (the term coined by one of the pioneers in transpersonal psychology, Richard M. Bucke)[11], or call it *participation mystique*, or call it nature mysticism, or call it unity consciousness, the bottom line is the same. We are not the center of the universe. We represent one cell in the living organism called the earth. This current manifestation represents just a blip on the radar screen of the earth's evolution. And this earth is one of many planets revolving around our sun. Our sun, in turn, is one of millions of suns in our galaxy. And our galaxy is one of millions of galaxies in the universe.

The mystic has a sense of both humility and awe around all of this. As an old rabbi once told me, everyone should carry two pieces of paper in their pocket at all times. One piece of paper should say, "I am nothing but dust and ashes." The second piece of paper should say, "The whole universe was made for me." Both pieces of paper are accurate and both messages are needed to keep us in balance. Whether we are feeling insignificant or incredibly valuable, however, the bottom line is that the mystic feels part of it all.

By the way, this might be a good time for us to define the terms "mystic" and "mysticism." As a seminary student in Rome, I was given a working definition of mysticism from the vantage point of religious orthodoxy. An old professor looked down the end of his pointy nose through his pince-nez glasses and told us, "Gentlemen, there are only two things you need to remember about mysticism. It begins in 'mist', and ends in 'schism'."

Hopefully, we can do a little better than that today. We need to, pardon the pun, demystify mysticism. What mysticism refers to is the process of going deeply into the ultimate meaning of things, the Great Mystery. (Hence mysticism.) One does not have to enter a monastery to do this. One simply has to see beyond appearances into the true nature of things. Anyone who does this is a mystic.

There is something transcultural and even transreligious about the experience. It is said, for example, that all mystics come from the same country and speak the same language. Their literal "language" is not the same. We have seen, in fact, how different the reporting can be. But the sense of unity, however one defines it, is one of the universal experiences upon which all agree.

2)Love – Talk about finding it hard to speak about the unspeakable! Love is the ultimate example, especially in the English language. In the Greek language, there are three main ways to define love: *agape* (love of God); *philia* or *storge* (love of humans as our brothers and sisters); and *eros* (erotic love). In the English language, we use the same word to refer to love of God, love of pizza, and love of baseball.

The modern day mystic does not use the term in that limited way. What is being referred to is a state of consciousness characterized by unconditional acceptance and feelings of positive regard for others. I almost hesitate to use the word "feelings", because there is nothing transitory about this state of consciousness. It is more like a shift in awareness based upon a perception of reality.

In this case, one senses a kinship with all creatures and a genuine appreciation for their value, even if the individuals cannot see this value in themselves. There is compassion, too. The word "compassion" comes from the Latin words "con" (with) and "patior" (to suffer). The implication is that you are truly sensing the other's pain and, in a sense, suffering along with them. This is not the same thing as co-dependence, where the boundaries between you and the other are forgotten and you are trying to live someone's life for them. Instead, it is similar to the attitude of the bodhisattva, a person who makes a conscious decision to incarnate time and time again until all human beings have been liberated from their prisons of self-rejection, based upon a distorted poor self-image.

Love is particularly important, or at least should be, for those who claim to follow Jesus. Indeed, if one were to try to classify him, Jesus could best be described as a sort of love mystic. He did not take the Hindu approach of starting the spiritual journey at the "chakra" (or center of consciousness) having to do with security, and working one's way up from there. Nor did he take the approach of starting with higher states of consciousness and allowing those states to "filter down". Granted, his personal prayer, the "Lord's Prayer" does seem to do this, but, in the context of his whole life, he seems to have taken the approach that we need to begin by opening up the heart to others. Love one another unconditionally, totally, without judgment, forgiving seventy times seven, and your spiritual growth will take care of itself.

If one were looking for a key to unlocking the possibility of a truly ecumenical approach to the human situation, agreeing on the need for love toward one another would be as good a place as any to begin. Granted, in Islam and Judaism, there is somewhat of a tougher edge in the approach, but it is still a form of love. This attitude of unconditional positive regard for others is so important that any spiritual growth without it is virtually impossible. To think that one can move forward spiritually while shutting down on the heart level is like expecting one's car to run after having put some sand in the gas tank. The car might chug along for a while, but it is only a matter of time before the car stalls out.

Some aspects of love – such as forgiveness – are a little more difficult to deal with. We have dealt at length earlier in the book with this concept. But let us again make the simple point that, without love, you may be religious and righteous and dogmatic and even correct, but you are not yet spiritual, and you are not yet free.

<u>3)Joy</u> – Consider the appearance and the demeanor of someone who has evolved spiritually. If they are the "real deal", there will be a joyfulness and a playfulness about themselves. They have learned to see life from such a broad perspective that they trust that "all is well and all manner of things will be well" (Hildegard of Bingen). They do not take themselves all that seriously. They can laugh at themselves and see all of life as *lila*, the Hindu term that means "the play of God."

Consider a couple of well known examples of this. How about Pope John Paul II using his cane as a hockey stick when he spoke to the youth of America? How about the ever twinkling eyes and soft, loving visage of the Dalai Lama? How about the playful, loving energy of Richard Alpert (known as Ram Dass) as he tells self-effacing stories in his role as a spiritual teacher? How about the mercurial, impish, magnetic energy of Mother Theresa?

None of these souls, along with countless unknown persons, who have tapped into a deeper reality, are living their lives in a stingy, restricted manner. They are living life big and it shows. This kind of joy in living cannot be faked or acted out. It is a spiritual quality that is either there or it is not there.

Some people confuse joy with pleasure or happiness. These qualities are related at times, but are very definitely not the same thing. Pleasure has to do with the satisfaction of the five senses. One can be sated with pleasure, positively orgasmic, but still be utterly without any joy. When the sensual stimulation ceases, one is back to the low level, chronic state of depression that perhaps was present before the sensual stimulation began. Sometimes joy may be felt in a sensual way in the body, but it does not work the other way in reverse. Sensuality can never produce joy. An example of joy overflowing into a bodily sensation comes from the movie <u>*Chariots of Fire*</u>. In trying to speak about the relationship of his running to his religious beliefs, the young Scot says, "When I run, I feel God's pleasure."

Joy is not the same thing as happiness, either. Happiness is more of a conditional state of mind. When things have worked out well for us, when things are going along smoothly, we say that we are happy. However, things change. We can find ourselves unhappy with our marriage, with our job, with our lifestyle. When circumstances change, we can find ourselves becoming an unhappy man or woman. Joy is more stable than that, less contingent upon external circumstances. We can be joyful no matter what is swirling around us. The presence of joy in a person cannot be simulated. It has nothing per se to do with being an extravert or having a manic personality. No, joy is something that transcends one's psychological type or one's personality. It is an expression of the soul, welling up from deep within, that is contagious and life-giving.

4)Peace – Another of the hallmarks of a spiritual state of consciousness is something referred to as peace of mind. This is not exactly the same thing as coming to terms with the circumstances of one's life. It goes much deeper than that. For a person may, in fact, be very unsatisfied with the circumstances of life, be they personal or public, yet still be centered and at peace.

As usual, let me give an example. Martin Luther King lived arguably one of the most tumultuous lives anyone can imagine. He went from crisis to crisis, from jail cell to jail cell, with his life under constant threat. He did his best work during the late 60's, finally being assassinated in 1968, the year of the death of Robert Kennedy and the year of the Kent State killings and the year of the infamous Democratic convention in Chicago. When those of us old enough to remember these events firsthand think about those times, many of us wonder how we and the world survived it all. It was hardly a peaceful time by anyone's definition. Yet there was Martin Luther King preaching nonviolence and love in the midst of it all. And there he was radiating an inner peace that could be sensed by all who saw him speak. His inner peace clearly did not stem from outer circumstances, nor did it flow from him living an orderly private life either. Indeed, reports of marital infidelities are only one example of the fact that his personal life had many contradictions and inconsistencies in it as well.

What seems to have been the source of King's peace is something that had relatively little to do with anything in the outer world. It seems to have come from a sense that he was in the flow, doing what he was put on this earth to do. His sense of mission (from the Latin *missio*, which means "being sent") enabled him to radiate a deep sense of peace, which came from being at "the still point of the turning world" (as T.S. Eliot put it in the *"Burnt Norton"* section of *Four Quartets*). Anyone who has seen TV footage of his speech the night before he was killed knows what I am talking about. Realizing that threats on his life were very real and to be taken seriously, Dr. King nevertheless proceeded to encourage his people to continue the struggle. As he did so, he had a look about him, not of the fiery zealot, but of a man who was carrying out a mission and a mandate that was larger than himself. He was doing what he needed to do and then was detaching from the results, even if this meant the end of his life on this earth.

This state of peace, then, has very little to do with the surface of things and everything to do with tapping into a reservoir beneath the surface. Once again, along with love and joy, peace cannot be faked. It cannot be bought with a million dollars, either. It is a byproduct of being in touch with a deeper aspect of reality, one that has its own rules and laws. If you have reached your center, then you have, as Saint Paul puts it, "that peace of God, which is so much greater than we can understand" (Phl. 4:7). When things are stressful or perhaps disintegrating all around you, when you have no business feeling okay, you just simply have this inner peace that comes from a trust that some power that is smarter than you and more powerful than you has everything under control and that everything will work out. It may not work out the way you had planned it or had envisaged it, but you have this sense, this conviction, that everything is working out according to some higher plan.

I realize that for those who have experienced these inner states of consciousness, no explanation is necessary. And for those who have never experienced these states, no explanation will suffice. To them, it all must sound like mumbo jumbo or some pop psychology. However, these states are real, universal, and, furthermore, capable of being replicated. How we go about the replication is something else entirely. For our purposes here, the point simply needs to be made that higher realms of consciousness exist and are accessible to those who seek them sincerely and courageously.

5) *Service* – Those who have tapped into the ultimate truth of who they are inevitably have a desire to serve others and to serve the world. Someone once told me that this world can be divided into two groups of people: givers and takers. Certainly, there is a lot of truth to this statement. However, I think it goes a lot deeper than that. When a person has experienced the ultimate truth of who they are, that person *automatically* then becomes a giver. So perhaps a better way to put it might be this way: This world is divided into two groups of people, those who are awake and those who are asleep. For, when people wake up, they always, without exception, have a desire to be of service. Once again, let me go back to Dr. Martin Luther King, who said, "When a person has been touched by the love of God, they have no alternative but to serve." Dr. King is expressing this truth through religious language, but the truth is a universal one, whether or not one espouses a religious philosophy. Being of service is part of our hardware, to use a computer image. It is not software, not optional, not culturally relative. Laws of the universe work that way. Finding one's center results in a desire to serve. It is that simple.

This is an important point to make because so many people are afraid that, if they pursue the spiritual path, they may tune out to reality. The common image of a spiritually evolved person is often that of a person with long hair, beads, and a vacant stare; or it is someone who is an "ozone ranger," a "space cadet," out of touch with the world, as we know it. In fact, nothing could be farther from the truth. Bogus spirituality might look like that. However, an authentic spiritual encounter sets a person free, with a consequent desire to do something meaningful with one's life. Fear no longer rules the day, be it fear of failure or – just as common – fear of success.

Let me give a few examples of how this works, one example from the sixteenth century and two from our times. The person from the sixteenth century who comes to mind is Theresa of Avila, a Carmelite nun who lived a contemplative, cloistered life. If anyone would be a candidate for dropping out of the daily fray, it would seem to be someone like her. But the deeper Theresa penetrated into the truth of things (and there is universal consensus about her being one of the giants of the spiritual path), the more practical she became. Rather than settling back in a mode of withdrawal, she became a tenacious activist and reformer. She took on the ecclesiastical powers as well as the civil powers, eventually being hauled before the Inquisition because of her radical ideas. She hired a lawyer to help her buy up properties that were to be used for her vision of what an authentic religious community should look like. She made an indelible mark on the society of her day, all the while spending several hours each day in prayer and reflection.

Someone from our century did a similar thing with his life, but he was even more controversial. I am referring to Thomas Merton, a Trappist monk from the monastery of Gethsemenae, Kentucky. I won't go into his odyssey as to how he decided on monastic life. You can read his own fascinating account of that in his book, *The Seven Story Mountain*. What is relevant to our discussion here is that his immersion into a spiritual perspective gave him a keen insight into the political movements of his day.

From his monastery cell, armed only with a subscription to <u>U.S. News & World Report</u>, he was one of the first in our society to predict riots in the ghettos of our cities. In addition, he became an astute critic of the Vietnam War, leveling a searing commentary on the flimsy logic trying to justify the war.

Merton's death remains one of the most mysterious events of those tumultuous times. On the one trip of any magnitude that he undertook away from his monastery, he was electrocuted by touching the wires of a fan while in Bangkok, Thailand. Much has been written about the theory that he may have been assassinated by the CIA. Certainly the CIA knew of his tremendous clout in shaping people's attitudes against the war. And they certainly knew of his much-publicized whereabouts. It is impossible to prove anything one way or the other about this matter, but that is not my point in citing this incident. The point here is that the very fact that we would even seriously contemplate this scenario proves the point that Merton's spiritual search did not take him away from this world in any significant way. Indeed, his perspective from behind the monastery walls seemed to make him an even more acute observer of the American scene, and perhaps even dangerous to some.

My final example of how spiritual insight makes one more practical and more beneficial to the world concerns a man who shall remain anonymous. His story is a simple one. Before having a spiritual breakthrough, he was an enormously successful and affluent businessman. Then he had a spiritual awakening that rocked him to his heels. After a period of disorientation, he went back to his business and was more affluent than ever. There was, however, one major change. Now he devotes the bulk of his work and his money to helping poor children from around the world. That is the way it works with an authentic spiritual breakthrough. You do not become less human; you become more human.

This calls to mind a well-known little story about spiritual growth called "The Woodchopper." The woodchopper says, "Once upon a time I used to be a woodchopper. And then I saw the light! So I became a person of prayer and meditation. But then I saw even more light. So now I chop wood again."[12] The simple point here is that, if the breakthrough is real, your life will become more real. Putting on a spiritual face, whatever that is, is not what it is all about. You will, in many ways, be the same person that you always were, but now you do what you do with greater freedom, joy, and generosity, and a sense of authenticity, a sense of True Self, which includes all creation.

6)Creativity – Finally, a spiritual breakthrough will result in a creative life. The opposite of depression is expression. When someone is living a life of chronic, low grade depression, all of their energy is spent on trying to make it through the day. When one has, to some extent, literally seen the light and felt the power and experienced the love, the individual often reports feeling like a co-creator with the Divine. The image often given is that of feeling like a channel. You are no longer the only reality in life. Plus, you no longer see yourself as the only resource, either. It is as if one feels like an instrument, serving a higher authority. There is more energy and ideas than ever. In addition, there is more willingness to make mistakes, to take chances, to fall on one's face time and time again. That is because the ego is no longer in the survival mode. It is in its service mode, reporting for duty every day to the True Self.

The creativity may express itself in writing, in organizing a soup kitchen, in dance, painting, sculpture, in organizing a protest march or a petition drive. Actually, the possibilities are endless. The point is that never more will your life be boring or even predictable. Like a nimble brush in the hands of a master artist, your life is constantly moving across the canvas of life, creating joyfully, endlessly, a never finished work of art.

Before one comes to this realization, however, one must do much searching, make many mistakes, go up numerous blind alleys, be humbled, broken, learn how to surrender, usually only after reaching one's personal rock bottom. With such a price tag, no wonder the spiritual path is "the road less traveled" (Robert Frost). But, although the cost is great, the payoff is infinitely greater. Being set free, finding one's center, is the most empowering, fulfilling experience that a human being can have. It is worth sacrificing everything else, absolutely everything else, in order to arrive at this state of consciousness. May you, the reader, discover this place within your soul and may that discovery liberate every aspect of your being. If this happens, you will be fulfilled beyond your imagination, and the world will have been enriched greatly by your presence.

CONCLUSION

Throughout this book, I have tried to keep a clear focus: explain in simple terms what it means to grow spiritually. In order to do this most effectively, I consciously chose to avoid, for the most part, philosophical and theological language. Instead, I chose the language of psychology. I did this because this is a language that most people understand. It is a language relatively free of dogmas. My purpose was to lay out the spiritual journey from the womb to the tomb. I wanted to demystify the process and to dispel many of the illusions that people have about spiritual growth.

It is now time to summarize and recap, once again in the simplest language possible.

1. The ego (or self) is divine and, therefore, perfect.
   (Chapter 1)

2. The newborn soul initially reflects that divine perfection.
   (Chapter 1)

3. Some wounding to the soul, most typically by its primary caregivers, causes the child to lose its sense of innocence. (Chapter 1)

4. There are many ways to be wounded, but they all result in the person feeling fear and a lack of safety. (Chapter 2)

5. This expulsion from our "Garden of Eden" results in a sense of alienation.
   (Chapter 2)

6. We then construct an artificial hybrid called a "survival personality" to help us deal with the pain of life.
   (Chapter 3)

7. Over time, the "survival personality," based upon fear, increases our suffering and alienation. (Chapter 3)

8. We then seek relief from our suffering through the use of money, sex, and power. (Chapter 4)

9. When that does not take away our pain, we often self-medicate by using substances or behaviors in an attempt to change our consciousness. (Chapter 5)

10. As we move into mid-life, we survey what we have done with our lives. We are disappointed, and this disappointment frequently leads to a depression (Chapter 6)

11. If our lives are "off-center" enough, our bodies may manifest an illness as a way to get our attention. (Chapter 7)

12. Our physical or psychological pain may be so great that we contemplate suicide. (Chapter 8)

13. Finally, we experience a breakdown of our old, limited sense of self. (Chapter 9)

14. This death of who we thought we were leads to the discovery of our true self. (Chapter 10)

15. The journey to wholeness entails forgiveness of those who have wounded us. (Chapter 11)

16. The ultimate challenge is for us to forgive ourselves and to reclaim the split-off parts of who we are. (Chapter 12)

17. As we grow in consciousness, we need to figure out how our primal instincts (especially anger and sexuality) fit in with our spiritual path. (Chapter 13)

18. Our growth in consciousness results in a transformed life more liberating than we ever thought possible.
(Chapter 14)

So now what? Well, for one thing, the journey begins all over again. The philosopher Hegel said that, in life, we begin with a thesis. Something then happens that causes us to totally reject that thesis. With time, the thesis and its antithesis merge into a synthesis. That synthesis then becomes our new thesis. It is the same way with our growth in consciousness. We begin thinking that we are a skin-encapsulated ego. We then reject that and become "spiritual". With time, we integrate our ego and our new consciousness and we think that this is the "new me." Surprisingly, this new thesis will then undergo the process all over again. But, each time, we are progressing into the evolution of our full potential: a person with Christ-Buddha consciousness who knows that the whole universe is sacred.

I have tried to describe what this consciousness looks like and feels like in Chapter 14. It is the greatest gift that life can possibly offer. Sometimes I feel like I could jump out of my skin with gratitude and bliss. To know in an experiential way that you are a divine being (along with everyone and everything else) is the most liberating thing that one can possibly experience here on this earth.

Perhaps it might be good here to clear up one final consideration: are we god or are we not? The answer depends on who is asking the question. If it is the survival personality who is posing the question, then the answer is: you *are* god, but it sure does not *feel* like you are god. But, if it is the true self, the authentic self, then we can say, along with Jesus, "The Father and I are one" (John 10:30).

We are not the Creator of the universe. To think so would be the height of grandiosity and self-delusion. But we are the Christ, the Buddha, and the incarnation of the Creator. Does not the child share the very same life as the parent? Of course. And we, as children of the Source, are made, not just out of star stuff, but also out of God stuff as well.

The world would look a lot differently if all human beings knew, really knew, that they were divine beings. It is to such a consciousness that the children of Earth are heading. We can either help it along or slow it up a bit but we cannot stop it. Why not surrender to the truth of your being? Some have said that we are afraid to face our weaknesses. Maybe so. But, as Nelson Mandela put it in his 1994 inauguration speech as President of South Africa,

"Our deepest fear is not that we are inadequate. Our deepest fear is that we are powerful beyond measure. It is our light, not our darkness, that most frightens us! We ask ourselves, who am I to be brilliant, gorgeous, talented, fabulous? Actually, who are you not to be? You are a child of God. Your playing small does not serve the world. There is nothing enlightened about shrinking so that other people will not feel insecure around you.

We are all meant to shine, as children do. We were born to make manifest the glory of God that is within us. It's not just in some of us: it is in everyone. And as we let our own light shine, we unconsciously give other people permission to do the same. As we are liberated from our own fear, our presence automatically liberates others!"

Nelson Mandela
1994 Inaugural Speech

The journey to wholeness began with divinity and ends with divinity. As the poet T.S. Eliot puts it, "And the end of all our beginnings will be to arrive where we started and know the place for the first time."

The *"Burnt Norton"* section of Four Quartets

We do not, then, need to *become* spiritual at all. We already are, always have been, and always will be divine beings. In that sense, the spiritual journey does not really take us anywhere else at all. It is just us waking up to the person that we have always been and just did not realize.

I would like to end with my favorite story. It is the story of the "Golden Eagle" that Anthony de Mello, S.J. tells in his book, <u>The Song of the Bird</u>. I will take the liberty of paraphrasing the story.

Once upon a time, there was a baby eagle that got separated from its mother at birth. The baby eagle was then adopted by some backyard hens. The backyard hens taught the baby eagle what they thought the meaning of life was. So the baby eagle learned to keep its gaze in the dirt, scratching and clawing, occasionally flapping its wings a little and lifting a few feet off the ground.

When the eagle grew up, it happened to look up in the sky one day and see this majestic figure soaring effortlessly through the heavens. The eagle then asked its adoptive parents, "Who is that?" "Ah," the parents said, "that is the golden eagle. He belongs to the sky. We belong to the dirt, because we are backyard hens." And so the golden eagle lived and died as a backyard hen because that is what he thought he was.

You and I live surrounded by a bunch of backyard hens – a few turkeys as well – who are always telling us that we cannot fly. They tell us to abandon our spiritual idealism and to do unto others before they do it unto us. We are told that we are nothing but protoplasm, produced by coincidence, with no purpose. Yet, despite these messages, there is a voice within us that keeps telling us that we are golden eagles with an eternal destiny. It is that voice that prompted you to read this book. Let us never abandon our destiny or our dreams. We are all called to soar with eagle's wings. Nothing less than that will ever satisfy the cravings of the human heart.

ENDNOTES

Chapter One

[1] Steven Johnson, <u>Character styles</u>, (New York: W.W. Norton & Co.).

Chapter Three

[2] John Firman & Ann Russell, <u>Opening to the inner child</u>, (Palo Alto, CA: Psychosynthesis Palo Alto), pp. 18-19.

[3] John Bradshaw, <u>Healing the shame that binds you</u>, (Deerfield Beach, FL: Health Communications, Inc.), pp. 17-19.

[4] <u>The American Heritage Dictionary</u>, (Boston: Houghton Mifflin Company), p. 129.

Chapter Five

[5] Robert Masters and Jean Houston, <u>The varieties of psychedelic experience</u>, (New York: Dell Publishing Co., Inc.).

[6] William Johnston, S.J., see <u>Christian Zen</u>, (New York: Harper Colophon Books) and <u>Silent Music</u> (New York: Harper and Row).

Chapter Nine

[7] Gerald O'Collins, S.J., <u>The second journey: Spirituality and the mid-life crisis</u>, (New York: Paulist Press).

Chapter Ten

[8] John Firman and Ann Russell, <u>Healing the human spirit</u>, (Palo Alto, CA: Psychosynthesis Palo Alto), Chap. IX.

Chapter Twelve

[9] Jung, C.G., <u>The Wisdom of the Dream</u>, Vol. 3, (Chicago: Public Media Video).

Chapter Thirteen

[10] T.S. Eliot, <u>Four quartets</u>, (New York: Harcourt Brace).

Chapter Seventeen

[11] Bucke, R., <u>Cosmic Consciousness</u>, (New York: E. P. Dutton)

[12] DeMello, A., <u>The Song of the Bird</u>, (New York: Doubleday), pp.16-17

Recommended Reading

Barnwell, F.A. <u>Meditations on the Apocalypse</u>. London: WH Smith Co.

Bucke, R. (1991). <u>Cosmic Consciousness</u>. New York: E.P. Dutton.

Bradshaw, J. (1988). <u>Healing the Shame That Binds You</u>. Deerfield Beach, FL: Health Communications, Inc.

DeMello, A. (1978). <u>Sadhana</u>. New York: Image Books.

DeMello, A. (1982). <u>The Song of the Bird</u>. Garden City, NY: Image Books.

Dychtwald, K. (1977). <u>Body-Mind</u>. New York: Jove Publications.

Eliot, T.S. (1974). <u>Four Quartets</u>. New York: Harcourt Brace.

Ferrucci, P. (1982). <u>What We May Be: Techniques for Psychological and Spiritual Growth</u>. Los Angeles: J. P. Tarcher.

Firman, J. and Russell, A. (1994). <u>Healing the Human Spirit</u>. Palo Alto, CA: Psychosynthesis Palo Alto.

Firman, J. and Russell, A. (1990). <u>Opening to the Inner Child</u>. Palo Alto, CA:

Psychosynthesis Palo Alto.

Grof, C. and S. (1990). <u>The Stormy Search for the Self</u>. Los Angeles: J. P. Tarcher.

Grof, C. and S. (1989). <u>Spiritual Emergency</u>. Los Angeles: J. P. Tarcher.

Hardy, J. (1987) <u>A Psychology with a Soul</u>. London: Arkana.

James, W. (1985). <u>The Varieties of Religious Experience</u>. New York: MacMillan (Original Work Published in 1902).

Johnson, S. (1994). <u>Character Styles</u>. New York: W. W. Norton & Co.

Jung, C. G. (1961). <u>Letter to Bill W.</u> Reprinted in <u>ReVision</u>, 10, 21.

Masters, R. and Houston, J. (1966). <u>The Varieties of Psychedelic Experience</u>. New York: Dell Publishing Co., Inc.

May, G. (1988). <u>Addiction and Grace</u>. Harper Collings: New York.

Merton, T. (1948). <u>The Seven Story Mountain</u>. New York: Doubleday and Company.

O'Collins, G. (1995). <u>The Second Journey</u>. Distributed by GraceWing, Morehouse Publishing: Harrisburg, PA.

-----------. (1984). <u>Pass It On</u>. New York: A. A. World Services, Inc.

Pearson, C. (1991). <u>Awakening the Heroes Within</u>. New York: Harper Collins Publishers.

Stevens, J. (1994). <u>Transforming Your Dragons</u>. Bear and Company, Inc.: Santa Fe, NM.

Vaughan, F. (1985). The Inward Arc. Boston: New Science Library.

Walsh, R. (ed.) and Vaughan, F. (ed.). Beyond Ego. Los Angeles: Jeremy P. Tarcher, Inc.

White, J. (ed.) 1995). What Is Enlightenment? St. Paul, MN: Paragon House.

White, J. (1990). The Meeting of Science and Spirit. St. Paul, MN: Paragon House.

Wilber, K. (1981). No Boundary. Shambhala Publications: Boston.

Yeomans, T. "The Three Dimensions of Psychosynthesis," Concord, Mass: The Concord Institute